Oct

Laurie & Drew!

All The Best!

Chris [illegible]

We are not alone
even in our solitude.

The Science of WATCHING, *the Art of* SEEING, *and the Power of* NATURE ABSORPTION

Chris Lewey
S.M. Fisher
J.K. Lounsbury

The Science of Watching, the Art of Seeing, and the Power of Nature Absorption

ISBN: 978-1-63381-380-9

Designed and produced by:
Maine Authors Publishing
12 High Street, Thomaston, Maine
www.maineauthorspublishing.com

Printed in the United States of America

For Paul, with gratitude

We were four siblings and together we traveled many trails and had numerous adventures throughout our childhoods and beyond. During our lives, both together and separately, we have learned through our varied experiences the importance and great value of the Power of Nature Absorption.

Now we are only three, but our brother Paul's knowledge, courage, wonderful sense of adventure, and deep spiritual understanding remain with us always as our adventures continue.

Yesterday the Tufted Titmouse started singing, and today I heard the first Chickadee "spring song," which seems a bit early—expected in February, but now still January. It was one of those days of "February" light—bright and warm—and bone-chilling temps in the shade. More glorious days to come, and the birds are the heralds.

Table of Contents

Foreword

There are many nature books that focus on identification—perhaps because names provide us with a sense of order. But as Benjamin Franklin once said, "What signifies knowing the names, if you know not the nature of things?" I'm sure that Ben Franklin would have embraced this eye-opening book by naturalist Chris Lewey, S.M. Fisher, and J.K. Lounsbury. *The Science of Watching, the Art of Seeing, and the Power of Nature Absorption* opens our eyes to new ways to appreciate the nature that surrounds us. Far beyond naming, this book is about discovering familiar features of the natural world such as wildlife, weather, wind, clouds, and night. The authors offer abundant new information about how to observe and enjoy nature near home. This compelling book also offers nature activities for children and adults and an inspiring collection of classic nature poetry.

I met Chris Lewey at the Hog Island Audubon Camp where for many years we taught adult birding and natural history classes. The legendary Hog Island Camp is all about experiential learning with a distinct flare for having fun in nature. In this spirit, Chris would sometimes dress in a full body gorilla suit and lope at a distance through the dark spruce forest. Amazingly, most people never saw him! His point was to demonstrate how much wildlife we miss seeing in nature!

In addition to learning how to observe, this book also offers a spiritual perspective about nature, leading the reader toward "Nature Absorption"—seeking ways to find harmony between our outer world and our inner world. The authors liken their book to a compass pointing toward an enhanced awareness of nature that can be experienced by everyone. They explain—"There is a divine living presence in the natural world that resonates with the living spirit within each of us, unveiling our own relationship with God." Yet the authors understand that "God" means something different to everyone, so they leave the spirituality element for each reader to discover on their own.

The field exercises for adults are aimed to reconnect us to nature. For example, activities titled: "Nature Absorption," "Nature Journaling," and "Bird Listing" offer ways that adults can practice Nature Absorption—a process that grounds people in the rhythm of nature while moving toward a more wakeful presence in the natural world. Activities for families also focus on this idea. Parents will be happy to find this collection of "Nature Encounters"—alternatives to the "technological tsunami" that entices children to stay indoors.

Finding ways for people of all ages to spend more time in nature has never been more important. There are more than 400 scientific studies that demonstrate how nature benefits our mood, psychological well-being, and mental health. Likewise, blood pressure, heart rate, and stress hormones all drop with time in nature. Recent research about memory shows that children raised in greener neighborhoods have more neural connections in brain regions tied to memory and attention. This research shows that bird watching is an especially good way to strengthen memory capacity. The repeated process of simultaneously assessing dozens of detailed field marks, habitat, sounds, and a myriad of other details necessary for quick identifications slightly thickens the brain's cerebral cortex as avian know-how deepens, creating capacity for better memory. This makes it easier for experienced birders to add new information to their mental repertoire. The growing science associated with more time in nature is so convincing that doctors in at least 32 states regularly prescribe visits to parks as nature therapy.

I hope these revelations about the health benefits from time spent in nature may encourage more people to spend time outdoors. These discoveries are timely as recent surveys indicate that 25 percent of U.S. residents spend less than two hours a week outdoors! Chris Lewey, S.M. Fisher, and J.K. Lounsbury have given us a timely tool for engaging people of all ages with new ways to enjoy nature. I hope more people will notice the wildlife around them and realize that they are part of nature. It's never too late to notice the "gorilla in the woods," learn the skill of Nature Absorption, and move toward a conservation ethic for taking care of our very special planet.

Stephen Kress,
Founder Project Puffin

Introduction

The Science of Watching, the Art of Seeing, and The Power of Nature Absorption

As coauthors and siblings, we have shared a lifelong common interest and connection with Nature Absorption. What began as separate voices merged into a project that took on a direction of its own. We had the same parents, we lived in the same household and shared many of the same experiences, yet each one of us has a different point of view. It couldn't be otherwise, as everyone sees the world from a different standpoint. The ancient parable of the blind men and the elephant illustrates the obvious tendency to claim conclusive truth of reality based on one perspective of a subjective experience, while ignoring others' perceptions that may be equally true, though also limited. By individually changing our perspectives, our consciousness, it becomes possible for each of us to *see* more of the elephant (reality) as a whole. "*Knowledge is structured in consciousness.*" —Maharishi Mahesh Yogi

Our original title for this book was *Birding with God and the Power of Nature Absorption*. However, it occurred to us that the word *God* could be misconstrued, according to each individual's personal outlook or belief. God has many names and no name. It is not possible to simply use the word *God* to describe the experience of God. The authors of this book, all three of us, would describe God differently. There are similarities, but we each have a unique experience and relationship with God. To *say* something is one thing but to *feel* it is something other. Our hope is that you, the reader, will put your own interpretation on the word God as you read through this book.

Nature Absorption is a path of intuition, healing, and spiritual transformation. We cite many voices from numerous ages, cultures and traditions to illuminate this truth. There are books that encourage a connection with Nature on many different levels, but this book makes connections with scientific facts and spiritual relationships that open us to a different perspective and enhances the awareness of the sacred all around us.

There is knowledge that can be taught, like history or geography, which instills an appreciation for and an understanding of the subject. But there is another kind of knowledge that can only be transmitted (in a similar way that light or heat is transmitted). It is this second type of knowledge that comes through affinity with Nature, that actually arouses an innate way of thinking, an opening of the heart. Nature transmits a subtle and potent energy that can be absorbed by us, Nature Absorption, bringing about physical, mental, and spiritual transformations. These changes lead to harmony and healing on multiple levels.

Rudolf Steiner makes the point that people long ago had a "*subtle feeling awareness*" of what is occurring in nature. They did not just notice autumn's colored leaves or spring buds becoming summer's flowers; they actually felt the atmospheric changes. "*Thus, the human being was inwardly intimately linked with the course of the year, so intimately linked that he had to say to himself: 'I know about what I am as man only when I don't live along stolidly, but when I allow myself to be lifted up to the heavens in summer, when I let myself sink down in winter into the Earth mysteries, into the secrets of the Earth.'*"

"*...man felt that he was not only an earth-being but that his essential being belonged to the whole world, that he was a citizen of the entire cosmos.*" —Rudolf Steiner

We can encourage this awareness in ourselves by being more conscious of, and having a wakeful presence in, the Natural World. Our mind intentionally chooses what it pays attention to. We are constantly being assailed with stimuli, and it seems the work of our mind is to choose what information it brings to our awareness, and what it keeps *hidden*. As a baby, then as a child, we gradually *learn* to restrict our awareness to only that which helps us function in our environment, reality as we interpret it at any moment. Much of the time, we are unconscious of this selection process, but sometimes a noise, an unexpected sight, or a strong emotion will come to our attention. Often when I'm driving a familiar route, I seem to be on automatic pilot, and it is only when I come back to an awareness of where I am, do I realize I was functioning but not really paying attention. I passed by numerous objects and people; I saw them, but I was not really conscious of them. However, when I am driving to an unfamiliar location and need to be vigilant about paying attention, I am more aware of what I see. When we want to, when we make an effort to, we all have the capacity to stay alert, to be aware; to be awake to the world around us.

Our awareness is naturally pulled toward more pleasurable stimuli. Our mind is *drawn* in that direction, *called* to a more enjoyable level. By opening ourselves afresh to the Natural World, we are capable of expanding our consciousness, increasing our awareness. We are not just observers; we become participants. Through Nature Absorption, there is a harmony between our outer world and our inner world. God is not distant from us. God's essence is in all of Creation and it is through God's energies that we can experience a living God, intimately involved in an ongoing relationship with each of us and all of Creation.

There is a malaise in our world today, a nervous imbalance caused by the excess of chemicals, technology, and world conditions; silence and stillness have become elusive for many. We are living in an age of anxiety, distracted by many things. People feel they are *beside* themselves. There is an overwhelming sense of being disconnected from ourselves, from each other, and from the world around us.

This book is simple, a compass pointing toward an enhanced awareness that can be experienced by everyone. We include practical, experiential exercises that encourage Nature Absorption. This is a simple, effortless experience that recalls us back to our Self, to a transcendent moment.

"There is a Divine living presence in the Natural World that resonates with the living spirit within each of us, unveiling our own relationship with God."

This spiritual connection with Nature is vital to our well-being. Through an emphasis on birding and ecology, along with some clear

Nature Absorption exercises, spiritual awareness is enhanced and amplified. One exercise, "The Science of Watching and the Art of Seeing" came out of a birding workshop developed while Chris was an instructor/director at Hog Island, Maine, a National Audubon camp for adult birders.

This book is designed primarily for adults, but we have added several "Nature Encounters" that work well for families of all ages. Children need time away from electronic devices and TV screens. Parents are continually seeking strategies to entice their children away from the harmful effects of a technological tsunami. It is important to have exposure to and time spent in this miraculous world in which we live. We all know the importance of fresh air, exercise, and sunlight, but a transformative awakening can be gained through Nature Absorption. These encounters, though simple, are enjoyable, informative, and beneficial for both adults and children.

A variety of photographs and poems have been included in order to enhance the experience of Nature Absorption. They present insights in a way that words alone cannot. Through potent word combinations and rhythm, poetry inspires imagination and triggers an emotional connection to what is occurring. Photographs, like poems, also make an emotional connection, arousing thoughts and feelings, but through the use of light rather than words. There is a simplicity in photographs, but an intricacy in what they convey. Photographs and poems shine a light on places in the heart revealing what otherwise may be elusive to the intellect.

This is a useful tool for birders, nature enthusiasts, travelers and anyone seeking to increase their knowledge, experience, and insight, going beyond *identification*. For example, birding books have evolved from identification guides to include behavior guides and books about ways to bird and becoming better birders, but this book is more about how *birding* can make a better *you*. Initially, travelers through this world don't see themselves as *pilgrims*, but become inspired with the realization of a new awareness, unveiling affinity with the Natural World around them.

SECTION I

Great Blue Heron

Chapter One

Birding with God

I first birded with God back in 1964; this avian connection with God began on weekends in the spring and continued through midsummer that year and beyond. I was eleven. I did not know at the time that *He* was there and involved, fully participating. Now I know, it is not all that surprising to look back and see that it could not have been any other way. It was the plan.

The Eastern Whip-poor-will sang his notes richly and clearly from his rock perch beside the Bungalow's side-porch and entered the premier position of being the first recorded bird on my life list. And so things began, not with celebratory trumpets of legions of angels, but with one small songster on the edge of a two-acre field, on the side of a little mountain, at the start of a summer now long past.

I did not have a field guide, did not know there was such a thing. I did not have any other information about this bundle of singing feathers. I only knew he was repeatedly calling out his name to me, "Whip-poor-will, Whip-poor-will."

God did not point out the Eastern Whip-poor-will. He did not explain its life history, nor discuss the migration that was looming in the months to come. He did not discuss the diet or the nuptial performances involved in being a Whip-poor-will. He was in essence this little Whip-poor-will and was singing his own glory to the night of lower Green Mountain.

I grew up just north of Boston, on the northern bank of Chelsea Creek, the trickling beginnings of the Chelsea River. This tidal flow separates the Boston suburbs of Chelsea and Revere. It swells quickly and flows into the Mystic River, which soon mixes with the Charles and becomes Boston Harbor, which hosts a rich history of busy shipping traffic and tales of the beginnings of our country. The traffic and narrative continue today.

Our home was in Revere, and our neighborhood hosted an endless flow of hide-and-seek, street-ball, tree-climbing and nonstop entertainment for any kid living in one of the nearby homes. There was not much in the way of rules: Don't get hit by a car or truck and be home before dark, that was it. Twilight was a favorite time. The afternoon of play fading to a conclusion often pushed the limit of sight until darkness saturated every inch of the street, the ball could no longer be seen, and friendly faces could no longer be recognized.

It was a world of houses orderly queued up on paved streets with granite-edged concrete sidewalks, parking lots, and backyards connected with fences and hedges. Bigger buildings clustered at the west end of neighborhood streets along Broadway: stores and shops, a granite-front bank, drugstore, post office, five & ten, pizza and sub shops, an Irish bakery, and an Italian grocery with sawdust on the floor along with the smell of fresh salami permeating both aisles. A favorite destination was Paone's Spa, a fruit, newspaper, and racetrack-program store with a standup fountain for nickel Cokes, frappes and root-beer floats and ten-cent double-scoop ice cream cones and a multilevel glass case filled with penny candy. Way at the back, across from the jawbreakers and licorice, was a wooden booth that was piled with magazines and fruit boxes, and never used for sitting. There were two twirling racks of comic books and another rack of pocketbook novels: Zane Grey's, Louie L'Amour's and Erle Stanley Gardner's. The purveyors were the wonderful Paone brothers (Joe, Charlie, Dom, and Sal) who always greeted me with a smile and the acknowledgment to onlookers of my being Paul Lewey's boy. My Uncle Brother (my dad's oldest brother) was often there with a folded race form marked up in pencil, with circled favorites and scratched-out losers, holding a potential win in hand. Most of the older men, the *paisans* of Broadway, called me "Paul," somehow thinking I was my older brother who had walked the same worn, wooden floorboards and prowled through those book racks fourteen years before me, thinking that my older brother never grew older. I assume that it fit into the timelessness of those days. Life seemed to crawl comfortably along Broadway and the other streets and backyards of Revere. This was one of my two worlds.

This life in the city was suspended almost every weekend with a three-hour drive to *the country*, our summer home on the Mountain Road at the base of Green Mountain in Effingham, New Hampshire. It was a different planet from the stone-and-brick buildings and paved sidewalks and backlots of Revere in the sixties. It was always an adventure just to travel that distance in a car that sometimes (that often) broke down and almost always blew a tire either on the Friday night trip north or on the Sunday late-afternoon return. This was very much like the early space flights: launch preparation, suspended adventures out of this world, followed by the return, recovery, and transfer back into the world of the ordinary, the world of after-school play in the quiet streets or connecting backyards of Pleasant Street. I lived two very different lives and seldom brought any friends into this weekend world. There was so much to fill the time, and I never understood the concept of boredom while saturated with the outdoors and blind to my divine birding companion's presence. Upon approaching the Bungalow, we would strain to be the first to see the white wooden gate at the base of the drive. "I see the gate; I see the gate!" was announced by one and then sung by all and we turned the corner by the big white pine and pulled up to the top of the hill. The car door opened, and I ran to the woods and was lost to the rambles of my brook for much of the remainder of the day and into my dreams through the night. I loved the brook. It was my brook, my rocks, my bridges, my explorations, and the clock would just stop for hours—timeless.

Each weekend I would be saturated with the smells and sounds of the uncultivated outdoors, intoxicated by the forest. Prowling the brook as far as I could, making my way deep into the woods or prodding the rocks and dead limbs of one pool after another. I knew each pool, each rock, each tree-root cave under bank: always changing, always the same. I built bridges over the water and crossed on fallen trees, jumped across in places, and hopped on unevenly spaced stepping rocks. The "brookies" (two-inch, native trout) and the insects (caddis and dragonfly larvae, black flies, and mosquitoes) were there in force and only a minor bother that never kept me from my brook.

It was refreshing to have a drastic change of pace, scene, routine or no routine at all—freedom! I remember clearly knowing the meaning of the word *freedom*—last day of fourth grade, a hot June day. The bell rang, and it was a run down the corridor, down a short flight of wooden steps, a landing, and another flight taken in two bounds. Both doors were open wide at the west end of the McKinley School. We burst through like a prison breakout onto the granite steps (over the wall!), sun bright overhead, a bit of salt in the air from an occasional whiff of ocean breeze—an east wind. I did not stop running until I was on the other side of Broadway, only slowing a bit to time the lights at the crossing, then speeding up halfway down Pleasant Street; we were heading to *the country*. We would spend the long days of summer either at "The Lake" or a few miles away in the cool woods of the Ossipee/Effingham line, with feet and hands combing every inch of the brook behind the house—adventures! Adventures to be had, adventures to be cherished.

And so it began…a journey of miles…of days…an adventure of emotions and spirit, and never did the thought of what would come to be ever cross my mind.

Without my noticing, through these repeated dips into the Natural World of the country, Nature Absorption was bringing about a profound change. Upon our returns from the country to the familiarity of Pleasant Street, I increasingly sensed that the large shade trees lining the street were somehow welcoming me home. My longing grew for the climbing tree of my backyard, kindred of the woods in the country. This huge White Spruce dominated the far corner. Through my adventurous climbs, I began to realize that this tree was a living being, and as I held tightly on to it, it was holding on to me. This individual spruce held me in its arms up at the highest point I could climb. From this lookout we both could see the whole yard below us, rose trellis and rock garden, and neighboring backyards beyond. A Blue Jay's view of these green oases amid the boards and bricks and pavement of the city.

Immersed in the rich world of Nature in the country, dipped and saturated as a dyed cloth, I was being changed experientially, a new awareness brought about through a change of perspective.

Not a cerebral interpretation, but an awakening of the heart brought about, not by following a set of beliefs or through scientific facts, but by experience. There is a Divine living presence in the Natural World that resonates with the living spirit within each of us, unveiling our own relationship with God.

There are many ways to encourage this.

Excerpts from "The Barefoot Boy"
—John Greenleaf Whittier

Oh for boyhood's painless play,
Sleep that wakes in laughing day,
Health that mocks the doctor's rules,
Knowledge never learned of schools,
Of the wild bee's morning chase,
Of the wild-flower's time and place,
Flight of fowl and habitude
Of the tenants of the wood;
How the tortoise bears his shell,
How the woodchuck digs his cell,
And the ground-mole sinks his well;
How the robin feeds her young,
How the oriole's nest is hung;
Where the whitest lilies blow,
Where the freshest berries grow,
Where the ground-nut trails its vine,
Where the wood-grape's clusters shine;
Of the black wasp's cunning way,

Mason of his walls of clay,
And the architectural plans
Of gray hornet artisans!
For, eschewing books and tasks,
Nature answers all he asks;
Hand in hand with her he walks,
Face to face with her he talks,
Part and parcel of her joy, —
Blessings on the barefoot boy!

Oh for boyhood's time of June,
Crowding years in one brief moon,
When all things I heard or saw,
Me, their master, waited for.
I was rich in flowers and trees,
Humming-birds and honey-bees;
For my sport the squirrel played,
Plied the snouted mole his spade;
For my taste the blackberry cone
Purpled over hedge and stone;
Laughed the brook for my delight
Through the day and through the night,
Whispering at the garden wall,
Talked with me from fall to fall;
Mine the sand-rimmed pickerel pond,
Mine the walnut slopes beyond,
Mine, on bending orchard trees,
Apples of Hesperides!
Still as my horizon grew,
Larger grew my riches too;
All the world I saw or knew
Seemed a complex Chinese toy,
Fashioned for a barefoot boy!

The Bungalow, Effingham, New Hampshire

"The sun shines not on us but in us." —John Muir

Chapter Two

Nature Absorption

Most of us live out our daily lives in a world removed from the energies and influence of the Natural World. The ancients were aware of these powerful energies in Nature and looked upon these phenomena as spiritual entities. The indigenous people, those who live close to the Earth, feel the forces they live among.

We live today with an abundance of technology; we have so much information available to us with the tap of our fingers. By merely learning scientific *facts*, we think we now *know*, but an awareness has been lost in the act of *labeling*. *Naming* is not the same as *knowing*.

Having the scientific facts, but also introducing the spiritual, opens us to a different perspective, an awareness of the sacred all around us. These kinds of insights jolt us to another place, moving us closer to a truth, a different reality of which we are an intrinsic part.

For instance, water: how basic to our lives. We drink it, swim in it, skate upon it, and are made of it (70 percent). Yet, we do not usually think about the magical properties that break all the rules. Water, like most compounds, gets denser and heavier as it gets colder, but only up to 4° C above freezing, it then starts to get lighter and expands and floats as ice. Water defies gravity and moves upward from underneath the Earth to bubble out upon the ground into what in other times and other places have been called healing springs and holy wells.

When we see the sun shining on water vapor in a frothy waterfall and see a rainbow form, that is actually a revelation to us, a revealing to our senses that there is more happening here than meets the eye. This wakes us up, arouses our awareness, causes us to pause and pay attention to the moment; there is much happening both within and without. We need to give ourselves the opportunities to take part in what is occurring. We need to be able to *savor*, to *taste*—this is a different way of knowing. Enter into the Natural World in order for the energies, the power of Nature, to enter into you.

> *"Feelings are to the soul, what food is to the body."*
>
> —Rudolf Steiner

This book will not introduce you to God; you already know him. It may, however, alter your awareness. It may expose a perspective that could sharpen your vision and allow for more clarity in what you see. It can nourish your appreciation of the Divine relationship that you are in. Our intent is to share some insights about our connection with Creation—what you need to know about Nature and what Nature already knows about *you*!

Birds have always provided wonderful insights for us watchers of the world. With every glimpse of a nuthatch that visits the feeder and then disappears back into the balsam and spruce, we are seeing a fragment of a massive, complex system of life of which we are so much a part. The watching of one individual can provide us with some entertainment. We look it in the eye. We relish its awareness and its aliveness as it is drawn in to the feeder for a little nourishment, our offering to this other world of wildness.

Occurrences in the Natural World provide us not only with enjoyable experiences but also with insights into the workings of the complex ecosystem that we call home. No great revelations need to arise from our observations. Each provides a piece of the puzzle of this fascinating Natural World that is so mysterious, so intriguing, nourishing, and sometimes startling. It changes us.

Paying attention to the rhythms of the world brings tremendous joy to many of us who continue to be fascinated by the workings of the planet. Whether it is the changing of the seasons or the crepuscular moments between day and night, there is always something very much the same and quite often something unusual that captures our attention. There can be comfort in the ordinary and exhilaration in something new or different. It is an exciting place here on planet Earth in many ways.

Why do these moments resonate in us? The simple answer is that we belong, and we feel welcome here. We do not always feel comfortable in our world today. Many among us feel disconnected, isolated, overwhelmed by the discord in our lives, and caught in the talons of everyday chaos.

This chaos of the world is often reflected within us. There is a remedy, a way to easily restore the order of Nature within our own lives. The solution is on the individual level, and this is where our attention should be. We can appreciate our true nature, who and what we really are.

Quantum physics reveals that we literally resonate with our surroundings. We can choose our surroundings and trigger a change within. As one tuning fork vibrates, it causes another nearby to respond harmonically. The Divine quality in Nature effortlessly resonates within our being and brings about a metamorphosis.

> *"All things are parts of one single system, which is called Nature; the individual life is good when it is in harmony with Nature."*
>
> —Zeno, 300–260 BC

There is a simple process involved in sharpening one's vision and increasing awareness of this Divine connection, our relationship with God…Nature Absorption.

In India, cloth was colored by dipping it into a vat of dye and placing it in the sun to dry. Most of the color fades, but some is absorbed into the cloth. Repeating this process over and over, the dye becomes colorfast and does not fade. This is how our relationship with the Natural World becomes fully integrated into our awareness.

Frequent visits into the Natural World will saturate us with this connection so that it is not totally lost even in the midst of much (worldly) activity and discord.

Our moments of being awake in the Natural World are experienced with increasing frequency when we allow ourselves the opportunity to let Nature draw us in. The feeling of well-being and sense of belonging that Nature breathes into us continue to nourish us and awaken awareness.

Birding is an exercise in Nature Absorption. A temporary dip into the divine dye of Creation that gets renewed and eventually saturates without being lost. Eventually having become saturated like the cloth, we each come to the realization that we are very much a part of Creation…we belong.

> *"For from Him and through Him and for Him are all things…"*
>
> —Romans 11:36

Black Elk, Lakota medicine man and spiritual leader, taught the importance of recognizing that everything is a manifestation of the Great Spirit. He is within all and yet transcends all. Once we know this in our hearts, reverence and affection will flourish. We will attain a genuine communion with the Great Spirit. Then, our existence and actions will align with His divine purpose.

Birders often walk familiar roads; at different times of the day, during different weather conditions and different seasons. However, even familiar roads can provide surprises. We are going down this road and there is no way to know what is around the corner. Take a breath and be ready for whatever we might encounter.

"Yearning"
—Rumi

There is a candle in your heart,
ready to be kindled.
There is a void in your soul,
ready to be filled.
You feel it, don't you?
You feel the separation
from the Beloved.
Invite Him to fill you up,
embrace the fire.
Remind those who tell you otherwise that
Love
comes to you of its own accord,
and the yearning for it
cannot be learned in any school.

"The Tables Turned"
—William Wordsworth

Up! up! my Friend, and quit your books; (phones, laptops, etc.)
Or surely you'll grow double:
Up! up! my Friend, and clear your looks;
Why all this toil and trouble?

The sun above the mountain's head,
A freshening lustre mellow
Through all the long green fields has spread,
His first sweet evening yellow.

Books! 'tis a dull and endless strife:
Come, hear the woodland linnet,
How sweet his music! on my life,
There's more of wisdom in it.

And hark! how blithe the throstle sings!
He, too, is no mean preacher:
Come forth into the light of things,
Let Nature be your teacher.

She has a world of ready wealth,
Our minds and hearts to bless—
Spontaneous wisdom breathed by health,
Truth breathed by cheerfulness.

One impulse from a vernal wood
May teach you more of man,
Of moral evil and of good,
Than all the sages can.

Sweet is the lore which Nature brings;
Our meddling intellect
Mis-shapes the beauteous forms of things: —
We murder to dissect.

Enough of Science and of Art;
Close up those barren leaves;
Come forth, and bring with you a heart
That watches and receives.

Turkey Vulture

Chapter Three

The Science of Watching and the Art of Seeing

The language of Nature is universal. It is nonverbal and perceived through all our senses, enhancing our innate awareness.

Our five senses convey information to the brain. For instance, we may see movement high in a maple tree, colors of red and white. Perhaps we can identify this bundle of feathers. We may have attached the name *Rose-breasted Grosbeak* to this object of our attention. Our brain has categorized it and matched previous knowledge with present experience. We know this member of the Cardinal family, its life history, its ancestry, and how and where it makes its living. The science of watching.

However, intuitive perception is a knowledge received through the heart. It is a consequence of an activity of the spirit. It is an active, creative process that unveils this resonating relationship between the observed and the observer. There is a profound connectedness. Awareness is expanded on a noncognitive level. We no longer *identify* this bundle of feathers, we *recognize* it. It is familiar, and there is a resonance.

For decades birders have used the terms GISS (GSS) and Jizz to describe a concept of bird identification. There are various opinions of the origins of these terms. Some attribute GISS (general impression of size and shape) to WWII aircraft identification training. This perhaps speeded up identification from the more time-consuming effort of mentally assembling parts (wings, engines, fuselage, tail), to an innate pattern recognition to determine the whole. Jizz is possibly a much earlier term implying the recognition of the subtle energy characterized by a particular family or species of bird. Regardless of the terminology, it is essentially the same concept, an overall Gestalt perspective, the whole being more than the sum of the parts.

> *"Intuition is the clear conception of the whole at once."*
>
> —Johann Lavater

Butter Hill Road, Chatham, New Hampshire

Two pathways lead to understanding. The first is a rational, deliberate and lengthy journey demanding patience and effort. The second, driven by imagination, is swift; akin to electricity's rapid flow. Imagination's power allows for instant comprehension, bypassing intermediary steps. The knowledge gained through this latter method is vibrant and dynamic, far surpassing the outcomes of mere intellectual analysis.

I remember as a child waiting for my dad to get home from work. He was usually on the 5:00 pm or 5:15 pm bus that stopped on Broadway at the end of Pleasant Street. When the time arrived, I would go to the living room window that provided a view of the entire street down to the corner (two-tenths of a mile measured by my Raleigh bicycle odometer). Several men always got off the bus. They all wore the same type hat, a dark fedora, and similar overcoats, the field marks of many dads returning home after work in Boston. I could immediately pick out my dad from the group as soon as he had taken his first step. How he held his head, his upright shoulders, his size, his particular bearing, the indescribable uniqueness of how he carried himself. Even at a mile away, I would have easily known that this one was *my* dad.

Familiarity is what dominated over the superficial *field marks* of coat and hat. No longer just identifying but recognizing. There is a fluid, active relationship. We all have this experience, seeing with the heart. Something internally resonates with something external. The more familiar we are, the less we make note of the obvious, but we need it both ways. We want to recognize the familiar while appreciating the details. This is a 200 percent experience, perception by both head and heart. The experience fully resonates. "We love the things we love for what they are."

This activity is no longer just an observation but becomes a transformative experience: like doors opening, a breaking through, freedom—escaping the limits of habit, mindset and static perception. This is *knowing* rather than simply being informed—the resonating innate activity of Nature Absorption. The Art of Seeing.

Nature speaks to us of spiritual mysteries, but it is an open secret, more poetry than prose. There are many paths leading to the opening of ourselves to this transcendent spiritual relationship. Birding is one easy, comfortable, efficient, and exciting way of Nature Absorption.

"Hyla Brook"
—Robert Frost

By June our brook's run out of song and speed.
Sought for much after that, it will be found
Either to have gone groping underground
(And taken with it all the Hyla breed
That shouted in the mist a month ago,
Like ghost of sleigh bells in a ghost of snow) —
Or flourished and come up in jewelweed,
Weak foliage that is blown upon and bent,
Even against the way its waters went.

Of dead leaves stuck together by the heat —
A brook to none but who remember long.
This as it will be seen is other far
Than with brooks taken otherwhere in song.
We love the things we love for what they are.

"It's not what you look at that matters, it's what you see." —Henry David Thoreau

Black Cap Mountain, North Conway, New Hampshire

Excerpts from "In the Heart of the Woods" —Alfred Noyes

The Heart of the woods, I hear it, beating, beating afar,
In the glamour and gloom of the night, in the light of the rosy star,
In the cold sweet voice of the bird, in the throb of the flower-soft sea!...
For the Heart of the woods is the Heart of the world and the Heart of Eternity,
Ay, and the burning passionate Heart of the heart in you and me.

The Science of Watching and the Art of Seeing—Field Exercise #1

There are many watchers of the world, but those who merely *look*, often do not actually *see*. They do not fully experience what is there.

This exercise will take a look at the tools and techniques of nature investigation. We will make use of the tools commonly used for nature study such as binoculars and field guides. We will apply some techniques for seeing better and understanding more in the field with an emphasis on the real skill of bird watching. We will then take a step past identification and touch upon how behavior watching can improve our awareness and sharpen our perception beyond the view of our binoculars. This is an active method of Nature Absorption.

One of the most exciting aspects of birding is behavior watching, or just watching. So often our attention is focused on identifying what we are looking at and not looking closer and beyond. Identification can be a double-edged sword. It provides only an entrance into this experience. Regardless of how much birding you have done, there is always more to be gained from watching. Identification as a tool can be used for further investigation and exchange of information, or it can obstruct and often terminate our connection with the subject. If you want someone to stop wondering about what they are looking at, just tell them the object's name, and a myopic nature investigator will feel the urge to move on to the next victim for their list.

This exercise is not designed to be a handful of cut flowers, but rather tips on creating your own bouquet. Focus on the mechanical aspects of recording, and this will improve the unconscious observing. With continued practice, adjustments, and fine-tuning, you can shape this to suit yourself.

This shift from birding identification to behavior watching will improve your identification skills tremendously, while enhancing both your *sight* and your *insight*: Watching and Seeing. The real benefit of this exercise is a change in perspective, a radiance and recognition of something within that is the same as that which surrounds. This is a living relationship that resonates. The ongoing value in this exercise is not just in the pleasurable physical activity or the intellectual satisfaction of a birding outing, but more about the effects that follow: dynamic, enduring changes to your perception. This activity will help break down some of our habitual boundaries that narrowly focus and often cloud our view of the world. This will be a provocative and rewarding exercise in Nature Absorption.

This exercise can be done on your own, with someone else or even in a small group.

Materials needed:

- notebook
- pencil/pen
- watch
- compass
- binoculars / scope
- field guides
- anything else to make yourself comfortable while sitting outside

Part A: The Science of Watching: the how, where, when…

1. Find a place where you can comfortably observe an individual bird that you would expect to remain in the area for a period of time (a place where a bird might be nesting, feeding, or loafing for about twenty minutes).

Do not choose an individual that is just flying overhead. Minimize your presence with binoculars or a blind; consider your influence.

Note: Suggestion for setting up your notebook worksheets.

- Divide into three vertical columns. Run a timeline down the left side. Enter the time from your watch occasionally, and later you can see the time and length of an event play out more clearly.
- Make observations in the next column and leave the last column for your interpretations and added references from Part B.

Time	Observation	Interpretation	Activity # Date Location

Figure 1 notebook worksheet

2. Sit and begin by recording circumstances surrounding your observation site: location, time of day (use twenty-four-hour clock), date, weather, and physical landscape surroundings. Include the ordinary as well as the unusual. This should be written as a lengthy, detailed, descriptive account of your observations. Include types of vegetation (field, shrubs, trees), temperature, wind, scents, near and distant sounds, animals, cloud cover, location of standing water / brook / stream / river, relative location of other people. Allow your awareness to expand in all directions. Include yourself in this as if someone else will be reading it. Draw a map if this is helpful in capturing the scene. Again, these are guidelines, and your techniques may change with continued practice. There is no right or wrong way to do this.

Note: It is important to keep descriptions separate from interpretations (which will come in Part B). Just write down your observations without inserting "feelings" or "emotions." You are the watcher.

Before going on to Step 3, close your eyes for a minute or two and just be present.

3. This bird you have chosen to observe need not be familiar to you. You do not need to know anything about this individual, not even its species.

Describe the bird: its color, size, shape, relative dimensions (length of wing compared to tail, bill length compared to head), bill shape, color or patterns or any outstanding or unusual characteristics of this one individual. Make a simple sketch.

Observe and record in your notebook all the activities of this bird. Describe behavior in detail, describe flight activity, and describe all interactions with other individuals and also any interaction with you (remembering to minimize your presence). Use your watch and record a timeline of any behavior (along the left column); later you can determine the time of a flight or time between vocalizing, etc. What direction and angle does it fly off from? What direction does it return from? What height is it flying up to and does this vary? What direction does it leave its nesting box or perch from and does this vary? Quantify...how long, how often, how many times, your approximate distance from bird in feet, estimate large numbers. Again, just record your observations without emotional input or speculation as to why or what is happening. (Watch your language...avoid using anthropomorphic terms.)

- **Develop a field-note shorthand** that can save you time instead of writing out full words.

- **Underline species names** when used.

- **Use banding code** for species name, usually the first two letters of the first and second name in the common name, or the first four if only one name.

- **Vocalizations:** Do your best to describe any sounds the birds are making. You can make a graphic description with variable lines of song patterns or calls.
  Songs: patterns repeated
  Calls: short, no pattern

Some connection to the song or call can be made to help describe and assist in remembering. Some kind of cerebral tag can be put on the song that will assist in storing and recalling.

- **Bird Song translated to words** are helpful:
  White-throated Sparrow—"Old Sam Peabody, Peabody"
  Barred Owl—"Who cooks for you, who cooks for you all?"
- **Birds that sing their names:**
  Phoebe
  Chick-a-dee
  Whip-poor-will
  Etc.

- **Bird songs/calls related to familiar sounds:**
  Northern Saw-whet Owl—truck back-up alarm
  Blue Jay—squeaky pulley of a water well
  Black-and-white Warbler—squeaky wheel
  Field Sparrow—bouncing ping-pong ball
- **Adjectives describing bird songs/calls:**
  American Robin, Rose-breasted Grosbeak—sing-song
  Orioles—whistle-like
  Thrushes—flute-like
  Grackle—harsh
  Northern Parula—spiral ascending
  Acadian Flycatcher—abrupt

- **Symbols:**

Draw lines, notes of music ♪♪, and the like. Try to imitate or describe the song or call.

Take an Active Part: use verbal descriptions, notes of music ♪♪, what it might sound like translated into words, phrases.

- musical notes
- wavy lines—up and down and long and short
- sounds—buzzes, whistles, chips, etc.
- words

Remember to keep descriptions separate from interpretations—just write down the observation without adding your own perspective of what you think might be going on with the vocalization. Be careful not to be anthropomorphic in your observation descriptions. Watch your language, reread and make sure your language does not slant your perspective.

Continue recording your observations until you see the bird's behavior repeating itself. Continue until you see a completion of the routine. Overall, this period of time should be for about fifteen to twenty minutes of watching and recording the bird's behavior.

Have patience in recording and take your time with the details.

Part B: The Art of Seeing: Interpretation, the why and the what for…

This part of the exercise can be done either in the field or following your field outing, back in your armchair with your feet up and coffee on the side table.

In this portion of the exercise, you will speculate and categorize the observations that you have made. Here you will comment on what you believe is happening with this individual you have observed and give these actions some interpretation based on your own understanding, knowledge, or research.

Make your comments on the right side of your worksheet beside your observations. You may calculate the times of events from your running clock notes.

The behavior of a bird answers the demands of that individual's habitat. Natural selection interprets the environment through organism design. Those individuals that fit well into their habitat and are successful in becoming adults are then capable of passing that success down to the next generation. Those that are less successful do not pass on those unsuccessful traits.

All behavior observed will be of one or two types:

- maintenance behavior: preening, hunting, foraging, eating, etc.
- social behavior: interaction with other members of the same species or other species or with another animal or with *you*—mating, nesting, territorial display, intraspecific, interspecific.

Pay Attention To:

- Feeding styles:
  - specialists vs. generalists
  - hawking
  - perch gleaning
  - sally gleaning

- Social behavior:
  - threat and appeasement displays (often at feeding stations)
    - gaping (beak open as if to bite)
    - wing opening, head lowering
    - attack fights are minimized because of appeasement postures, i.e., hunches
    - shoulders, lowers beak, turns away
  - caution displays and vocalizations in the presence of a predator or human observer
    - erect posture, tail flicking, bill wiping
  - mobbing
  - flocking provides protection while feeding (also can be a site for information exchange), during migration, roosting at night
  - freezing, holding still
  - calls, both sexes
  - songs
  - courtship displays, nesting behavior
  - courtship feeding
  - mounting and copulation
  - nest building
  - incubation
  - egg turning
  - brooding
  - nest clearing
  - carrying food
  - distraction displays
    - broken wing/limp

After careful observation, one can often see predictable patterns develop and play out.

There can be a variety of interesting behaviors to record or ordinary repetitive behaviors can be seen as increasingly significant in your interpretations.

Your non-anthropomorphic descriptions of the bird's behaviors, with no motives or values involved, will help you to see more clearly what is happening and possibly transcend misconceptions that may have developed and been passed on about behavior. For example, "V-formation" flight behavior was once thought to conserve energy and gain lift from the bird in front, but this is now believed to not be the case, as the birds do not fly close enough to aerodynamically gain anything from their flight mates. This allows one to now speculate what the purpose might really be. It is possibly vision related (seeing all others in front), avoiding collisions flying in a group with a particular direction in play. This is an example of how an observation can be misinterpreted and easily shaped, directed, or misdirected by observers' biases and choice of words, subconsciously influencing the accurate interpretation of the experience. Assumptions based on previous beliefs in some cases turn out to be inaccurate.

This exercise in Nature Absorption can be seen graphically in this chart. Fig 2.

Knowledge is Structured in Consciousness

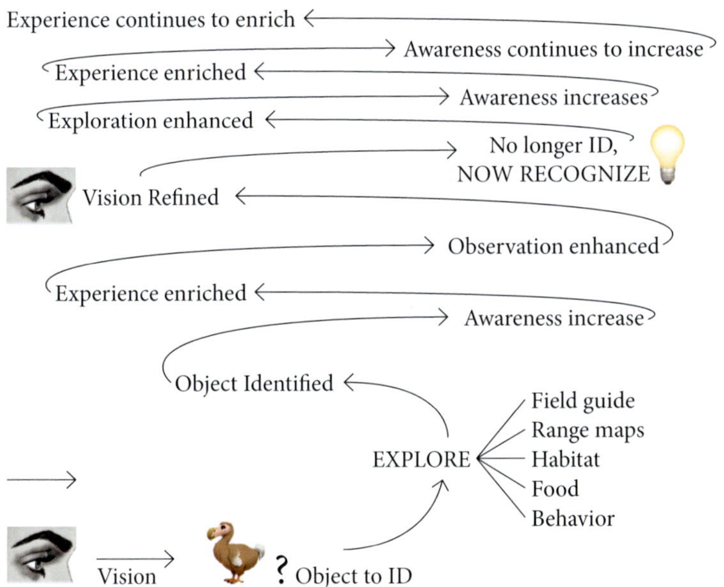

In our exercise we begin by focusing our attention, observing, and recording details. The observations are then investigated, identified, and interpreted based on our own understanding and amplified with information from field guides and other sources.

This exercise increases our understanding and expands our awareness by enlivening our experience and enhancing our observations. Vision is refined and future observations are then influenced by a new perspective.

This is an evolving, spiraling change in relationship with Nature. *Knowledge is structured in consciousness.*

A Childhood's Happiest Moment

It was springtime 1946. I was four years old. For the second winter in a row, I had been sick in bed for four long months with rheumatic fever. I remember one particular day soon after I was pronounced recovered and allowed to be up and about. I was standing in the kitchen with my jacket on, and my mother was kneeling in front of me struggling to pull on brown rubbers over my shoes. I was very excited and begged her to please hurry.

Mama had told me that it was a beautiful day and that, for the first time since my illness had sentenced me to my lengthy confinement and inactivity, I could go outside and play. I was thrilled. I knew my seven-year-old brother was playing in the yard with some of our neighborhood friends.

Finally, I was ready. Mama took me down the back hall and opened the door. I stepped out onto the top of the back steps. I immediately felt embraced by the sudden warmth of the intensely bright sunshine and the blowing of a gentle east wind. I was enveloped and caressed by the sweetest fresh air I had ever remembered. It filled my lungs and infused my entire being. I was held there in utter blissful joy and contentment. I was totally at peace. I remained there, silent in that moment. I was consumed by a deep sense of welcome and belonging.

Soon the noisy voices of the children in the yard ceased when someone yelled, "Look who's here!" They called my name and ran gleefully toward me. I did not make a sound nor resist as they took both my arms and gently drew me down the steps and into the yard.

> *"Now I see the secret of making the best person: it is to grow in the open air and to eat and sleep with the earth."*
>
> —Walt Whitman

"Sunrise on the Hills"
—Henry Wadsworth Longfellow

I stood upon the hills, when heaven's wide arch
Was glorious with the sun's returning march,
And woods were brightened, and soft gales
Went forth to kiss the sun-clad vales.
The clouds were far beneath me; bathed in light,
They gathered midway round the wooded height,
And, in their fading glory, shone
Like hosts in battle overthrown.
As many a pinnacle, with shifting glance.
Through the gray mist thrust up its shattered lance,
And rocking on the cliff was left
The dark pine blasted, bare, and cleft.
The veil of cloud was lifted, and below
Glowed the rich valley, and the river's flow
Was darkened by the forest's shade,
Or glistened in the white cascade;
Where upward, in the mellow blush of day,
The noisy bittern wheeled his spiral way.

I heard the distant waters dash,
I saw the current whirl and flash,
And richly, by the blue lake's silver beach,
The woods were bending with a silent reach.
Then o'er the vale, with gentle swell,
The music of the village bell
Came sweetly to the echo-giving hills;
And the wild horn, whose voice the woodland fills,
Was ringing to the merry shout,
That faint and far the glen sent out,
Where, answering to the sudden shot, thin smoke,
Through thick-leaved branches, from the dingle broke.

If thou art worn and hard beset
With sorrows, that thou wouldst forget,
If thou wouldst read a lesson, that will keep
Thy heart from fainting and thy soul from sleep,
Go to the woods and hills! No tears
Dim the sweet look that Nature wears.

Crawford Notch from Mt. Willard, New Hampshire

"You will go out in joy and be led forth in peace; the mountains and hills will burst into song before you, and all the trees of the field will clap their hands."—Isaiah 55:12

Chapter Four

Changing Perspectives

Imagination: (noun): the faculty or action of forming new ideas, or images or concepts of external objects not present to the senses.

Albert Einstein's perspective was that the true sign of intelligence is not knowledge but imagination. Imagination being more important than knowledge. He believed knowledge is limited, whereas imagination embraces the entire world. It has been said that *logic* will get you from A to B, however, *imagination* will take you everywhere.

No matter where we are, Nature is there, all around us, within and without, seeking our attention. We need a different perspective to hear this calling. A change of perspective leads to a change in perception.

The Natural World (including man of course) provides a great playground for our thoughts and ideas. It is like the game show *Jeopardy*...the answers are given and the questions need only to be asked. The answers are all around us, the products of millions of years of trials, with the successes leaving the failures to fall by the wayside. Living organisms are the products of what works and the result of what has been dropped off in the wake of all the attempts to better answer the demands and pressures of the surroundings. If we add the fact that the surroundings are in continual change, then we have a fluid and dynamic interplay that makes for the exciting world in which we live and seek to appreciate. An organism's challenge is to capture energy more efficiently than another energy grabber that is going after the same resources, not only at the same moment but over the span of generations. This provides for an exciting play of strategy and insight... of tools and techniques...of life and death...creation and dissolution. A wise man once told me that the only thing that is *not* changing in this world is the fact that everything is *constantly* changing...*everything* is changing except the constancy of ever-change.

Our investigations into the Natural World can be twofold. First, with a direction given to our awareness, we become more insightful to the happenings of the world. Second, the act of investigation itself can also expand our awareness and make us more efficient in our activity and experience, thus increasing our ability to see the world the way it really is, with all its exciting and close-knit connections. These connections range from relationships between species to the relationships between individuals; from animals to plants, from organisms to cells, from molecules to atoms...to stars and beyond. It is all a wonderfully complex, and at the same time miraculously simple interplay. As our insightfulness grows, we realize how very much connected *we* are. We are already there; we just have to see the connections to fully appreciate our richness.

> *"The eye sees only what the mind is prepared to comprehend."*
>
> —Henri Louis Bergson

Only the boundaries need to be removed and the barriers broken for our vision to become increasingly more clear. In an attempt to break boundaries, one's awareness sometimes needs to be wrenched in an alternate direction from its normal downstream course. I want to make sure that we agree about a few basic things, a simple foundation before going on. How we see the workings of the world matters. Perhaps then we can begin making some changes in our perspectives.

For example, let me ask, were you awake before the sun came up this morning? Were you alert? Were you up and out of bed? Wondering what the day had in store for you? What the plan of the universe was and how it was going to be laid out before you? Whatever time you got up, was it still dark? Were you up before the sun, or did you actually see the sun come up? In what direction did you see the sun come up? In what direction would you say the sun comes up *every* morning? In the east? Regardless of where you are, would you say the sun always comes up somewhat in the east? If not this morning, would you say that you have at some point in your life seen the sun rising in the east?

Probably you would say you have seen it set many times. As the day draws to an end, where would you look to see the sun go down, in the west? Our lives play out through the long bright days of summer into the long dark nights of winter, year after year. Would you say you have seen the brilliance of our closest star, some ninety-three million miles away, rising in the east and setting in the west?

If you answered "yes" to any of the above questions, then you are deceiving yourself.

We all know this has never actually happened for any of us: not today, not yesterday, not tomorrow. It never will happen. Not for you, not for me, not for anyone on this planet.

The sun does not come up in the east, shoot across the sky, and drop behind the western horizon. Although this is how we look at the world, picturing that the sun shoots up in the east and moves up and across the sky, until it somehow beckons from overhead that we should take our noon meal, and then by end of day it drops into some obscure place in the west. We all *know* this to be untrue, but even with this understanding, we often live our lives and relate our experiences and our conversations to this artificial model. We know the Earth is spinning and the sun is relatively stable. It does not come up over the horizon, then shoot across the sky and drop behind the skyline to our west. *Earth* rotates, dips and spins creating this effect only in our distorted perception. It is the planet's spinning that exposes the sun every morning.

Our falsely-based assumptions, though we know them to be without foundation, become the basis of our view of the world. Our perspectives can be made more realistic through our investigations and discussions into the workings of Nature, the world, the solar system, and beyond. We just need to take the correct angle and allow our perception to dive deeper into the way things really work, unclouded by our preconceived and often artificial foundations. There are many things like this that affect our perspective.

> *"The secret is to be awake. To be awake is everything. Keep awake whatever you are doing! Do not imagine that you are already awake. No; you are asleep and dreaming."*
>
> —*The Green Face*, Gustav Meyrink

There is great value in removing these limits and unveiling more reality. There is a reconstruction of a different perspective. In these moments of increased and heightened awareness, we wake up. Let's look forward with fresh eyes, Nature has much to reveal to us.

As some say,

"There are only two ways to live your life. One is as though nothing is a miracle. The other is as though everything is a miracle."

Journey into the world of Nature, the world of the obscure, the world of the ordinary, the world of ourselves and our awesome planet and see what it may hold. You can choose…the miracles are happening now…we are very much a part of them.

Food for thought…. The food on our breakfast plate is not typically seen as "packaged sunlight," but that is precisely what it is. We run on solar energy. We are solar powered.

"Nature's peace will flow into you as sunshine flows into the trees." —John Muir

Let's take a closer look at a green leaf and see what is going on. What we are looking at is an incredible piece of machinery. This is a tool, produced in the spring, which the tree puts out to capture energy from the sun. It is a solar collector. A leaf is designed to capture energy from a star that is over ninety-three million miles away from us. Even at the speed of light, it takes eight and a half minutes for that sunlight to reach planet Earth. It is captured by green plants and stored in nutrients that they get out of the soil and the atmosphere and from which they build carbohydrates. Those blocks of sugar are later broken down into energy used by the plant, or the sugars are consumed by anything that eats the plant. The process of photosynthesis is the production of food, not only for the plant, but essentially for everything that is alive on the planet.

In the ancient oceans of the world, the technique of trapping solar energy and bundling it into glucose was a clever idea developed long before we came up with the tongue-twisting term of *photosynthesis*. Single cells independently floated their solar panels in the direction of our closest star, all those millions of miles away, and managed not only to catch the light but to profitably pack it away in nutrients taken out of the sea, soil, and air. Later, this starlight could be unleashed and put to work producing more tiny energy grabbers. This turned out to be a profitable trend, and these early plants successfully passed on this miracle of *star-grazing* to their descendants. Subsequent generations enhanced the design, shaping the process to stages where some of these "light gatherers" joined forces and aligned into a better position to be more efficient solar collectors of the sun. These solar-packaging factories invested their profits in building more collectors as the Earth twisted and turned toward the incoming solar rays. Some even put this energy into wood production, lifting more and larger solar panels high above other grabbers and into more wind (carbon dioxide) and more sun.

Woody plants made progress and marched across the countryside, and soon huge forests claimed much of the land. The march continues, and plant succession is easily seen, still happening in fields and hills, on mountains, and in our own backyards.

White Oak, Mt. Auburn Cemetery, Cambridge, MA
"Every nature object is a conductor of divinity..." —John Muir

The pioneering lichens with algae-fungi teamwork had the unique ability to occupy barren rock, special forces engaging a challenging substratum: hard, slick, nutritive poor, and foothold challenged. Taking the high ground and maintaining a difficult occupation of bare rock, these early pioneers spread slowly in inhospitable territory. Their gains exceeded their losses…marginally. They broke rock into a more hospitable terrain and provided the mosses the opportunity for approach. These moist, successful, verdant designs (the second wave, reinforcements) trapped soil and smoothed the land. They provided a comfortable foothold for taller plants to sink their toes into. Mosses have to get their moisture externally. They lack the vascular design for water and nutrient transport.

Plants with plumbing can grow taller and be somewhat remote from their water source, only needing to get their feet wet occasionally. This is a great advantage in elevating solar collectors above the forest floor into more sunlight and carbon–oxygen breezes.

Rock and vegetation

"If you would understand the invisible, look carefully at the visible."—Talmud.

Young Sir Isaac Newton experienced the product of these complex structures while sitting under an apple tree. He pondered a falling apple and came up with perspectives on the universal force of gravity. I believe Newton, however, missed appreciating the real miracle of the moment. The question he easily could have asked was not why the apple was falling, but how it got up there in the first place!

The sophisticated water transport systems of plants defy gravity and provide even the tallest of trees a sip of nourishment at their very tips, sometimes well over three hundred feet above the forest floor.

Mosses are shadowed by grasses and sedges and these give way to taller annual plants that are succeeded by perennials. With a ploy of prudence, this year's sunlight is stored for next year's engagements. This starch-storing wave marches in for lengthy occupations. The pioneering Aspen and Birch take stand in sunny, open areas and eventually grab much of the incoming radiance, depriving their own seeds of the suitable bright nursery that once was there. Shade-tolerant hardwoods of Ash and Maple grow quickly. The broad leaves of these deciduous trees soon let very little summer light escape to the forest floor, eventually making the way for even

Fallen elder

more shade-tolerant species of evergreen spruce and fir to sprout. The offspring of these primeval species do very well in the darkened forest understory where they wait until an opening presents itself: a fallen elder, a flood of light, and a charge upward to join mature ancestors standing firm in changing and challenging seasons.

As the flora progresses, so does the fauna, and at each level a diverse host of animals (including man) complement the changing vegetation. Spiders and insects roam the terrain of lichen-covered rock in search of nourishment, much the same as the Moose and Black-capped Chickadees do in their meanders through Balsam and Red Spruce… an Earthly dance of field and forest, a quest for stored starlight.

And here *we* stand today on the same chunk of rock, still on course around ol' Sol, making our own occupation…it is the same story still unfolding. The sunlight from the star overhead flows as energy through our bodies. We are reconnected to the sun with every new breakfast that starts each day; our stomachs know, but our eyes often do not see past the menu. We run on star fuel; we drink the light of the sun; it flows in our blood. We are what we eat. We are starlight.

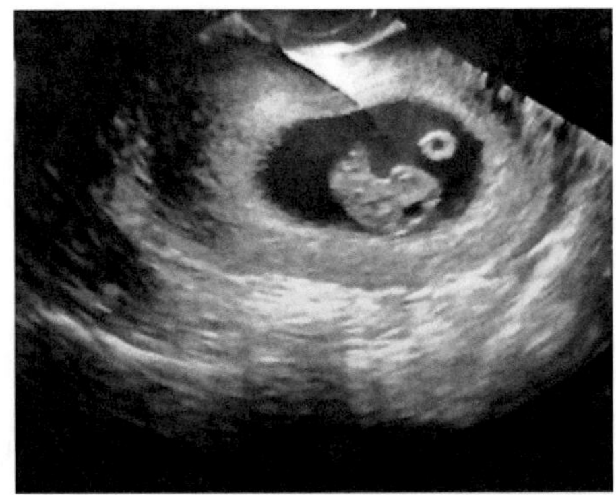

Fetal ultrasound "nebula"

Not only is our energy gleaned from a star, but the nutrients that we are made of also have their origins in the stars. The oxygen, carbon, calcium and iron making up our bodies were created in massive, collapsing stars. We are truly threads in the fabric of the cosmos.

Amazingly, we have all had the opportunity to *see* ourselves from outer space. Magnificent images of Earth taken from space stun us with the beauty of that glowing blue orb wrapped in swirling white veils. This is no longer simply earth; this is the Earth, a living being. Changes in perspective always awaken awareness. Gaia, the primordial Greek goddess, Mother Earth, has reemerged in our consciousness.

Why a goddess? Why the feminine attribute? Earth draws into herself forces from the cosmos, nourishes and nurtures within, and then brings forth all of life. Earth gestates and Heaven inseminates.

NASA image, Gaia

> *"I am a child of Earth and starry Heaven, but my race is of Heaven."*
>
> —Orphic Burial Tablets

> *"For in Him we live, and move, and have our being…for we are also his offspring."*
>
> —Acts 17:28

Hog Island, Maine

"The Day is Done"
—Henry Wadsworth Longfellow

The day is done, and the darkness
    Falls from the wings of Night,
As a feather is wafted downward
    From an eagle in his flight.

I see the lights of the village
    Gleam through the rain and the mist,
And a feeling of sadness comes o'er me
    That my soul cannot resist:

A feeling of sadness and longing,
    That is not akin to pain,
And resembles sorrow only
    As the mist resembles the rain.

Come, read to me some poem,
Some simple and heartfelt lay,
That shall soothe this restless feeling,
And banish the thoughts of day.

Not from the grand old masters,
Not from the bards sublime,
Whose distant footsteps echo
Through the corridors of Time.

For, like strains of martial music,
Their mighty thoughts suggest
Life's endless toil and endeavor;
And to-night I long for rest.

Read from some humbler poet,
Whose songs gushed from his heart,
As showers from the clouds of summer,
Or tears from the eyelids start;

Who, through long days of labor,
And nights devoid of ease,
Still heard in his soul the music
Of wonderful melodies.

Such songs have power to quiet
The restless pulse of care,
And come like the benediction
That follows after prayer.

Then read from the treasured volume
The poem of thy choice,
And lend to the rhyme of the poet
The beauty of thy voice.

And the night shall be filled with music,
    And the cares, that infest the day,
Shall fold their tents, like the Arabs,
    And as silently steal away.

"The Dawn Wind"
—Rudyard Kipling

At two o'clock in the morning, if you open your window and listen,
You will hear the feet of the Wind that is going to call the sun.
And the trees in the shadow rustle and the trees in the moonlight glisten,
And though it is deep, dark night, you feel that the night is done.

So do the cows in the field. They graze for an hour and lie down,
Dozing and chewing the cud; or a bird in the ivy wakes,
Chirrups one note and is still, and the restless Wind strays on,
Fidgeting far down the road, till, softly, the darkness breaks.

Back comes the Wind full strength with a blow like an angel's wing,
Gentle but waking the world, as he shouts: "The Sun! The Sun!"
And the light floods over the fields and the birds begin to sing,
And the Wind dies down in the grass. It is day and his work is done.

So when the world is asleep, and there seems no hope of her waking
Out of some long, bad dream that makes her mutter and moan,
Suddenly, all men arise to the noise of fetters breaking,
And every one smiles at his neighbor and tells him his soul is his own!

Sunrise, Chatham, New Hampshire

"The breezes at dawn have secrets to tell you
Don't go back to sleep!
You must ask for what you really want.
Don't go back to sleep!
People are going back and forth
across the doorsill where the two worlds touch,
The door is round and open
Don't go back to sleep!"—Rumi

"The Salutation of the Dawn"
—from the Sanskrit

Listen to the Exhortation of the Dawn!
Look to this Day!
For it is Life, the very Life of Life.
In its brief course lie all the
Verities and Realities of your Existence;
The Bliss of Growth,
The Glory of Action,
The Splendor of Beauty;
For Yesterday is but a Dream,
And Tomorrow is only a Vision;
But Today well lived makes every
Yesterday a Dream of Happiness, and every
Tomorrow a Vision of Hope.
Look well therefore to this Day!
Such is the Salutation of the Dawn

Renaissance

I was fourteen and a freshman in high school. We lived in Revere about a mile from my grandparents' home, the home I had spent my early childhood in, the house I never wanted to leave.

It was mid-February when we learned that Papa was ill. With no warning, our fit and active maternal grandfather, in his mid-seventies and with only a slight pain in his back, was diagnosed with terminal liver cancer, and given three months to live. Immediately, we moved back into the house on Pleasant Street so our mother could help our grandmother care for him.

I clearly remember hearing the news of Papa's serious illness. While I knew it must be true, I could not quite believe or accept it. In that death-sentence pronouncement, there was no room for hope that he might recover. There was no time in which to grapple with such a devastating loss. Three short months, and the days were already melting away.

A cold, numbing sensation with a dark, inner silence and fragility gripped me. I found myself in a place I had never been before—a kind of limbo hovering between disbelief and refusal to accept the reality that I was seeing every day. My wonderful and treasured grandfather was rapidly slipping further and further from his strong and agile self into a weak and frail shadow of what he had once been.

I automatically began to help my mother and grandmother in their loving, daily care of Papa. He never lost his soft-spoken, gentle, and kind manner. He was still Papa, a wonderful patient and always so appreciative of everything done for him.

As usual, I went to school every day. It was a very short walk through the priest yard of the church next door and across the intersection of Beach Street and Winthrop Avenue. School was a large, three-story, brick building on the corner. I then came straight home to take up my role as "helper" that I had voluntarily assumed. However, the strange sense of frozen emptiness still remained. It seemed as though part of me had become paralyzed. I went through the everyday motions of things, but I was somehow disconnected from my own internal self and disconnected from everything and everybody else. I was totally alone. I did not muse over these things. I did not consider or think about them in any way.

Time passed much too quickly, yet, at the same time, dragged on and on too slowly until one Saturday morning in late May. Papa was taking his last breaths, and our sorrowful family was close beside him. I stood beside a doorway in his room which was open to another room. My back was pressed against the wall as far from his bedside as I could get and still remain in the room. I had never been with anyone dying before, and no one so very dear to me had ever died.

Then it was over. No breath on the mirror Uncle held near Papa's face. I turned and flew out of the room through the open doorway beside me. I passed through one room and then into another. I was sobbing now. I found myself in my parents' bedroom at a second-story window facing up the length of Pleasant Street toward Broadway. I was staring out the window through my tears, when suddenly I received a tremendous jolt, an electric shock that shattered something deep within me. I felt I had been punched hard in the stomach. I felt sick, and I grasped my body with both my arms. I had been struck by a burst of startling color and light. Like Dorothy opening her black-and-white door to the dazzling colors of Oz, I could not believe my eyes. The beautiful maple trees, lining the street on both sides, were full with bright green leaves dancing in a gentle, spring breeze. The neighboring lawns were green. There were flowers growing and bushes in bloom. Birds were chirping and the sun was dazzlingly bright. The street was alive with the light and movement of late May.

I was shaken to my core. The last time I had looked, this street had been silent, still and gray with the barren, snow-covered chill of late February. I had completely missed the coming of spring. For three months, I had been blind to the Natural World around me. I could not believe it. Now it was warm and bright. The Earth had turned and the seasons had changed while I had remained frozen in place.

The shock had reconnected something in me, and I began to feel the pain, the agony of loss. I realized that my Papa was gone, and I felt as if there were an empty place in my heart and in my life where he had been. Life for me would never be the same, but I had begun the journey back from wherever I had been. I began the long process of grieving a loss that I had never even imagined could happen.

When we are disconnected from ourselves, we are disconnected from the Natural World. When we are disconnected from the Natural World, we are disconnected from ourselves. For we truly are one with the Earth and with the entire Cosmos.

Black-capped Chickadee

"The Winter Bird"
—Jones Very

Thou sing'st alone on the bare wintry bough,
As if Spring with its leaves were around thee now;
And its voice that was heard in the laughing rill,
And the breeze as it whispered o'er meadow and hill,
Still fell on thine ear, as it murmured along
To join the sweet tide of thine own gushing song.
Sing on—though its sweetness was lost on the blast,
And the storm has not heeded thy song as it passed,
Yet its music awoke in a heart that was near,
A thought whose remembrance will ever prove dear;
Though the brook may be frozen, though silent its voice,
And the gales through the meadows no longer rejoice,
Still I felt, as my ear caught thy glad note of glee,
That my heart in life's winter might carol like thee.

Nature Journaling—Field Exercise #2

The act of physically writing, moving pen or pencil on paper, creates a subtle experience of involvement that goes beyond simply recording an observation. Writing involves the senses and recognizes the texture and feel of pen and notebook. This act stimulates the brain and increases awareness, facilitating the retention of the observation. The observer now becomes a participant.

It has been said that writing by hand is a form of drawing, which is a creative activity usually involving the right side of the brain. Sketching can also be used to augment this process. Engaging the right brain more helps bring about a change in our perceptions; thus, a change in perspective.

Nature Journaling enhances our awareness of our natural environment. It causes us to stay alert, awake, and conscious of the world around us (both of typical and unusual happenings). We become more adept at watching and seeing the subtle changes that occur every day. As the world turns, each of our days is different from the day before. Everything has changed to some degree as we hurl through space, tilting either toward or away from the sun.

How to Journal? Any way you want—there is no right or wrong way.

Nature Journaling is, in a way, like keeping a captain's log, noting in a *book* your daily observations of the Natural World and your connections with it. If possible, keep a handwritten journal rather than typing your sightings and thoughts into a computer.

Your journal entries may be simple and brief sometimes and longer and more detailed at other times.

Feel free to include your emotional responses as well.

Example: "Dark clouds blowing in from the west as I was coming home—very ominous looking. We may be in for a storm."

Some simple suggestions:

1. Begin each entry with date, day and time (2/25/20—Tuesday 9:30 a.m.)

   You may be making one or several entries in a day.

2. Observe and record such things as:
   - Weather

   Example: "Beautiful day—cool, crisp (45°) deep-blue sky, fair-weather clouds over the mountains—bright March sun. The days are obviously getting longer now. Yippee!"

   Record such things as:
   - temperature
   - cloud formation
   - things typical & atypical for the time of year, and so forth

   - Wildlife seen or unseen

   Example: "Lots of birds at the feeders, mostly juncos and jays—saw a pair of cardinals on the deck this morning—Spectacular! The red squirrel wasn't here again today." Unusual—"Saw a chipmunk on the deck—should be hibernating."

   - Trees and other vegetation

   Example: "The sap is running—maple-sugar time has begun—a little early this year. Earlier this a.m., bare branches of the trees were heavy with last night's snow. The evergreen boughs were bent low. Now much lighter as the sun is bright today. On my way home, I noticed that the sun shining through those trees on the hill on Oak St. cast beautiful, long shadows down the hill."

- Any experiences, encounters, thoughts, and feelings relating to your nature observations that day.

  Example: "I climbed Kearsarge today, partly cloudy, cool, quite windy as we approached the summit. Magnificent view—visibility good. Had lunch on top—didn't want to leave. Found delicious blueberries along the path."

- Stop, Look, Listen, and Record

Now pick out a notebook that appeals to you and a pen that feels good in your hand.

Soon you will have a collection of messages from the person you were yesterday.

Beaver lodge winter

Beaver lodge summer

Chapter Five

Earth Breathes the Seasons as God Rings the Changes

"Earth Breathes the Seasons"
—J.K.L.

Feel Earth's great inward breath in autumn.
The closing off; the letting fall; the dropping down
There is a slowness and a cooling; the darkness drawing in.

With powerful strength Earth holds her breath,
and locks it deep inside. Winter sleeps quiet and cold.
Submerged in the depths of solitude, enfolded in stillness dark,
the gems of silence lay.

Earth begins to exhale, pushing up and out;
A rising upward, flowing out, warming toward the Sun.
The lifting and the lightness, the "Ah" of spring's release.

Earth wide open, breath entirely poured forth.
Out to the fullness of the heat and light; the Sun, the stars and beyond.
Surging skyward with music and dancing and colors profuse;
Summer's ecstasy.

Each respiration a cycle of the year.
There is a flowing down into the Earthly and a rising up into the Cosmos.
For child of Earth and child of Heaven
There is a leaving, a departing; but there is also a return.
We can lay in the grave and not perish.

> *"Rhythm and harmony find their way into the inward places of the soul."*
>
> —Plato

All of life is in a state of movement, a constant contraction and expansion, and it is in movement that rhythm is found. Our heartbeat and our breath are constant reminders of life's pulsing rhythms that move within and around us. We push air out of our lungs; however, it is the pressure of the atmosphere that fills us with fresh air. We are *inspired*; we are breathed by the sky around us. The moon waxes and wanes, the tides ebb and flow, the Earth rotates and the seasons change.

The phrase "ring the changes" comes to mind when thinking of the well-ordered constancy of Earth's daily and yearly variations. In bell ringing, each patterned order of striking the bells is called a "change." In order to "ring the changes," all the variations of a striking pattern are rung, bringing the ring back to its starting point; starting and ending on the same tone.

There is harmony in this song that Nature is singing; and just as a poem's rhythm resembles the emotion it arouses, when we are in the midst of Nature, our pace is set to its tune. The sounds, the air, shades of color, sunlight, and shadow—all find an echo within us and become a wellspring for body and soul.

Let's take a closer look at some of what transpires as God rings the changes of the seasons.

We will begin in autumn, using Northern New England as our backdrop. There is much happening, seen and unseen, on many levels during this exciting transition period. We have to remember, when we take a close look at New England, that there are only three months of summer. Twelve short weeks for all the vegetation to get their leaves out, capture the energy from the sun, and produce as much food for themselves as they can before they go through that long, dormant period of winter. These organisms have to come up with different strategies to deal with the different environmental pressures that winter will force upon them. Fall is a time of preparation.

The major problem for a tree to get through the winter here involves water management. Botanists describe Northern New England as a desert throughout the winter months. Technically it is a "physical desert." Some plants come up with a strategy to retain moisture. If they lose water in the winter months, they cannot replace the moisture since all liquid water is now locked up in snow and ice, unavailable to them. They employ tactics that are comparable to strategies that we find in desert plants. The most challenging day in winter for these trees is not a subzero, blustery, snowy day, but a warm, sunny one. If the trees warm up, they lose moisture and have no way to replace it.

Orchard

No orchard's the worse for the wintriest storm;
But one thing about it, it mustn't get warm.
'How often already you've had to be told,
Keep cold, young orchard. Good-by and keep cold.
Dread fifty above more than fifty below.'" —Robert Frost

"Good-by and Keep Cold"
—Robert Frost

This saying good-by on the edge of the dark
And the cold to an orchard so young in the bark
Reminds me of all that can happen to harm
An orchard away at the end of the farm
All winter, cut off by a hill from the house.
I don't want it girdled by rabbit and mouse,
I don't want it dreamily nibbled for browse
By deer, and I don't want it budded by grouse.
(If certain it wouldn't be idle to call
I'd summon grouse, rabbit, and deer to the wall
And warn them away with a stick for a gun.)
I don't want it stirred by the heat of the sun.
(We made it secure against being, I hope,
By setting it out on a northerly slope.)
No orchard's the worse for the wintriest storm;
But one thing about it, it mustn't get warm.
"How often already you've had to be told,
Keep cold, young orchard. Good-by and keep cold.
Dread fifty above more than fifty below."
I have to be gone for a season or so.
My business awhile is with different trees,
Less carefully nourished, less fruitful than these,
And such as is done to their wood with an ax—
Maples and birches and tamaracks.
I wish I could promise to lie in the night
And think of an orchard's arboreal plight
When slowly (and nobody comes with a light)
Its heart sinks lower under the sod.
But something has to be left to God.

Paper Birch trees

Robert Frost would often talk about another wonderful tree in the northern woods, the Paper Birch. These trees have a technique for keeping themselves cold in the winter in order to survive. The Paper Birch has stark white bark to reflect the warm sunlight that bounces off the snow. These are the trees the natives would strip the bark from and then stretch it over a wooden frame of White Ash to build their birchbark canoes.

During the summer, the forest is dominated by green chlorophyll, the main ingredient of photosynthesis. However, in autumn, we see two separate strategies being unveiled, the deciduous and the evergreen.

Since broad leaves give off moisture, deciduous trees must rid themselves of their leaves or risk losing their moisture during the winter. If they become dehydrated, they will not survive until spring. These trees separate themselves from their leaves by sealing them off. The leaves lose the summer green, unveil their autumn color and eventually drop to the ground. The oranges and reds of the Maples,

Autumn Leaves
"How beautifully leaves grow old. How full of light and color." —John Burroughs

the yellows of the Ashes and Birches, and the browns of the Oaks are exposed. These pigments, previously dominated by the green chlorophyll, are revealed as the chlorophyll is used up and can no longer be replaced in the leaf. This is the deciduous strategy.

These trees go bare through the dormant period of winter. In the spring, they need to rebuild. Deciduous means to cut off, to drop off. Dentists refer to our first set of teeth as our deciduous teeth. We replace them with permanent teeth. The antlers on Moose and deer are deciduous and fall off each autumn, unlike *horns* of some mammals that are permanent. This deciduous strategy works well for the bulk of the trees in the forest at the lower elevations here in New England.

On the other hand, primarily across the upper elevations, we see the evergreen strategy: a totally different approach to deal with the same problem, a lack of available moisture. These trees do not drop all their leaves. They have a different design. Their leaves are designed to retain moisture. Sometimes they are in the shape of a needle, long and thin, with a waxy cuticle and a thick rind; with the gas-exchanging stomata located on the underside of the needle, protected somewhat from the sun and wind. These trees are able to hold onto their leaves throughout the dormant winter months when all the deciduous trees are bare and holding onto their moisture.

These evergreen trees compete very well with deciduous trees. They can grow at much higher elevations where conditions are too harsh for the broadleaf trees. They are able to save all the energy it would take to rebuild their foliage in the spring. Also, they get a big head start photosynthesizing because they can begin the process when liquid moisture first returns to the ground, long before the deciduous trees. The broadleaf trees usually need the whole month of May just to rebuild their leaves.

More is going on with the deciduous strategies than meets the eye. All broad leaves work in much the same way. In a previous chapter, we went into some detail about the importance of these amazing solar collectors. However, this wonderful device is useless once we get into temperatures below freezing. Very quickly, all of the moisture will freeze, expand, and rupture the cell walls. When the cells lose their integrity, they become a great source of water loss for the tree. Therefore, these trees must drop their leaves. They need to become deciduous, and that is exactly what they do. It is a simple process. As the days get shorter and shorter, there are hormones that are produced in the tree that cause a layer of corky cells (at the base of the petiole, the stem of the leaf where it attaches to the tree) to swell and choke the leaf off, like a tourniquet. There is no longer any moisture passing from tree to leaf or leaf to tree. Anything that is in the leaf now cannot get over the barrier of corky cells and vice versa. Photosynthesis continues until all the chlorophyll is used up, but now it can no longer be replenished. We begin to see what the broad leaves look like when the green is taken away.

The yellow xanthophyll, the orange carotenes, and the brown tannins can now be seen. These pigments are present in the leaf all summer long and aid in the process of photosynthesis by trapping different wavelengths of light. However, the green of the chlorophyll dominates when present. When the green has been used up, the underlying colors are then exposed. In some species, as time goes on, the red mahogany color of the anthocyanins starts to migrate in as a result of sugars being broken down in the leaf and not being able to be eliminated.

It is the length of day that triggers the transition; not the cold. However, local environmental conditions can influence the intensity of the color. Depending on the temperature or the time of the day at which the plant, or a portion of the plant, receives sunlight can influence the transition and depth of color. This happens very quickly under the right conditions. The color can change from day to day, from hour to hour, depending upon these local conditions or environmental factors; these include sun, temperature, exposure, heat or cold, dry or moist, the genetics of the plant, and the plant's location in the local topography.

American Beech in winter

What a miraculous process this is! What intelligence the trees are expressing—they know exactly when and how to do all this! When we know the *wonder* of what is happening around us, we become more acutely aware. As we increase our awareness, we develop a deepening appreciation of the *wonder* of life itself. We begin to see with new sight—a change in perspective. We begin to perceive how *closely* we ourselves are woven into this "tapestry," into the very fabric of the entire Natural World.

Some deciduous trees like the Oaks and Beech, along with the Witch Hazels and Hornbeams, have an interesting characteristic. They will often hold onto their leaves all winter long, even after they have withered. These trees are identified as being "marcescent," a term that means to wither. These are the broadleaved trees in New England that one can see holding onto their dehydrated leaves after all the other trees have dropped their leaves. Sometimes after a strong wind blows, these leaves can be seen scurrying like little mice across the crusty snow. So, if you are in New England in the winter and you see a tree that has leaves on it, then you know it must be one of this small marcescent group.*

Also, here in New England, we have a species of tree that uses a unique strategy. This is a tree of many names: American Larch, Tamarack, and Hackmatack, *Larix laricina* in the Pine (*Pinaceae*) family. This tree has needles *and* drops them in the autumn, a deciduous conifer. Having the advantages of needle water conservation, it becomes deciduous for further benefit. This allows it to grow in marginal habitats that could be prohibitive for many species. It can grow further north than our other trees because of this strategy.

---

*Section II Making the Woods Your Own—A Retelling of an American Indian Legend

American Larch

"Inscription for the Entrance to a Wood"
—William Cullen Bryant

Stranger, if thou hast learned a truth which needs
No school of long experience, that the world
Is full of guilt and misery, and hast seen
Enough of all its sorrows, crimes, and cares,
To tire thee of it, enter this wild wood
And view the haunts of Nature. The calm shade
Shall bring a kindred calm, and the sweet breeze
That makes the green leaves dance, shall waft a balm
To thy sick heart. Thou wilt find nothing here
Of all that pained thee in the haunts of men
And made thee loathe thy life. The primal curse
Fell, it is true, upon the unsinning Earth,
But not in vengeance. God hath yoked to guilt
Her pale tormentor, misery. Hence, these shades
Are still the abodes of gladness; the thick roof
Of green and stirring branches is alive
And musical with birds, that sing and sport
In wantonness of spirit; while below
The squirrel, with raised paws and form erect,
Chirps merrily. Throngs of insects in the shade
Try their thin wings and dance in the warm beam
That waked them into life. Even the green trees
Partake the deep contentment; as they bend
To the soft winds, the sun from the blue sky
Looks in and sheds a blessing on the scene.
Scarce less the cleft-born wild-flower seems to enjoy
Existence, than the winged plunderer
That sucks its sweets. The massy rocks themselves,
And the old and ponderous trunks of prostrate trees
That lead from knoll to knoll a causey rude
Or bridge the sunken brook, and their dark roots,
With all their Earth upon them, twisting high,

Breathe fixed tranquility. The rivulet
Sends forth glad sounds, and tripping o'er its bed
Of pebbly sands, or leaping down the rocks,
Seems, with continuous laughter, to rejoice
In its own being. Softly tread the marge,
Lest from her midway perch thou scare the wren
That dips her bill in water. The cool wind,
That stirs the stream in play, shall come to thee,
Like one that loves thee nor will let thee pass
Ungreeted, and shall give its light embrace.

Everything in the forest is preparing for winter. Many of our birds migrate at this time of year. For example, in the fall the warblers leave the North and head south. They make this movement at night. Most small birds migrate at night to avoid predation by the hawks that migrate during the day. They can also feed during the daylight hours and store energy for another night flight. This nocturnal travel allows them to orient by the stars; they use celestial navigation! Studies in planetariums show that these migrants use certain star clusters, so flights can take place on some partially cloudy nights. Many of these birds, tiny bundles of life, weigh in at less than ten to twelve grams, less than half an ounce (about four dimes' worth of feathers…small pocket change). Some birds travel down into the Caribbean, and some to Central and South America. In some cases, this means a flight of over five thousand miles. Some of them negotiate the Gulf of Mexico, a nonstop flight over open water that takes place over a period of eighteen to thirty-six hours. These exceptional navigators also have the physical skill to endure this long migration. Of all the birds that nest in these northern latitudes, about 75 percent use this migration strategy. This is not an easy way to avoid the northern winters…70 percent of these populations are lost somewhere along the way through a variety of causes including age, light pollution, lack of food, and predation. Only the strongest fliers and best navigators complete the roundtrip, winning the opportunity to nest and pass their genetic strength down to the next generation.

Waterfowl

"To a Waterfowl"
—William Cullen Bryant

Whither, 'midst falling dew,
While glow the heavens with the last steps of day,
Far, through their rosy depths, dost thou pursue
Thy solitary way?

Vainly the fowler's eye
Might mark thy distant flight, to do thee wrong,
As, darkly seen against the crimson sky,
Thy figure floats along.

Seek'st thou the plashy brink
Of weedy lake, or marge of river wide,
Or where the rocking billows rise and sink
On the chaféd ocean side?

There is a Power, whose care
Teaches thy way along that pathless coast, —
The desert and illimitable air
Lone wandering, but not lost.

All day thy wings have fanned,
At that far height, the cold thin atmosphere;
Yet stoop not, weary, to the welcome land,
Though the dark night is near.

And soon that toil shall end,
Soon shalt thou find a summer home, and rest,
And scream among thy fellows; reeds shall bend,
Soon, o'er thy sheltered nest.

Thou'rt gone, the abyss of heaven
Hath swallowed up thy form, yet, on my heart
Deeply hath sunk the lesson thou hast given,
And shall not soon depart.

He, who, from zone to zone,
Guides through the boundless sky thy certain flight,
In the long way that I must trace alone,
Will lead my steps aright.

Not all of our birds are long-distance migrants. We have some short-distance travelers. The Canada Geese that nest inland do not go very far, only to the coast. The climate is milder there, with less snowfall, and they can find more to feed on. The ocean tempers and delays the seasons.

The Great Horned Owl does not need to migrate because these birds feed on mammals, and in the Northeast, terrestrial mammals are nonmigratory. Owls are primarily nocturnal hunters. They fly through the North Woods as silently as smoke, pouncing upon their unsuspecting prey from behind. Their talons are about the size of a man's clenched fist. These tools and skills make them successful, stealthy predators that are undeterred even by the defensive Striped Skunk, one of its primary objects of prey.

Snowy Owl, Back Cove, Portland, Maine

The Arctic-nesting Snowy Owl is less of a nocturnal hunter, being more active during the day. We do not have this diurnal hunter all year round in New England. He is a visitor from the North. This owl comes down during the winter months and finds it easier to locate food here; feeding on mammals and other birds.

All New England terrestrial mammals live here year-round, so they need to come up with strategies to deal with the change of seasons. Some of the strategies are rather interesting. Most of the mammals here are nocturnal, active mostly at night. There are only a few diurnal mammals, such as the Eastern Gray Squirrel and the Red Squirrel. They are active all winter long, running around during the day finding food, hiding food, and finding food that they have already hidden. This technique works pretty well for them. Our

Bobcat, Chatham, New Hampshire

Snowshoe Hare, Moll's Rock, Umbagog Lake, New Hampshire

chipmunks are deep sleepers, like our black bears, and only come out occasionally when conditions are good.

The Snowshoe Hare is resourceful. In late August a little dab of white can be seen between his eyes and ears. By the time the snow flies, he will be mostly white. Changing to a white color is a great advantage. With a white background of snow, the hare will be camouflaged. A greater advantage of this white coat is that each piece of hair lacks pigment. The central hollow shaft is filled only with air rather than pigment. The air is a much better insulator than the pigment. Being endothermic, like all mammals, they produce their own heat. That heat just needs to be conserved. The white coat, with all that air, is much warmer than the brown. In spring a new coat of cooler brown hair grows in for the summer months replacing the white hollow hair. It is a successful strategy. Winter or summer, they only need to spread the toes of their snowshoe-shaped feet and outrun the Eastern Coyote, one of their chief predators.

Eastern Coyotes differ from Western Coyotes in several ways. The Western subspecies weigh between fifteen and thirty pounds, whereas the Eastern subspecies weigh about twice as much, forty to fifty-five pounds. They are a large canine and have somewhat replaced the wolf that used to inhabit the Northeast. New England no longer has any wolves.

Unfortunately, many people did not understand the value of predation. Many still do not understand how important it is to have predators in the forest. The wolves were hunted to extinction. They were shot, they were trapped, they were even driven to hilltops and the hills were set on fire. This completely eliminated this population of a very much-needed type of predator in the forest. Coyotes migrated east above the Great Lakes through Canada, possibly mating with wolves along the way. This may account for their offspring being larger than today's Western Coyote. They somewhat took over the niche that was left vacant by the elimination of the wolf. This predator, larger and more robust than the Western Coyote, continues to be shaped by the demands of the challenging Northeastern Forest. We are fortunate to have such a healthy population of these successful predators in the forest here. They keep the forest healthy.

White-tailed Deer do not have any glamorous strategy; they just get fat in the summer months and into the fall. Then they rely on those fat reserves to get them through the winter. They end up feeding on apples throughout the fall. It is rather comical to watch as they stand on their hind legs and stretch, reaching the lower branches of an apple tree. It is to their advantage to gain as much weight as possible because very little is available to them in winter. They end up feeding on bark, which is low in nutrition. It is easy to tell when a deer has been browsing on a tree, as the teeth marks all go in an upward direction. Deer only have lower incisors. All members of the deer family only have front teeth in the lower jaw, so they have to strip the bark upward. They are the only mammal that does this. It is a fairly easy sign to interpret as you walk in the woods.

The largest member of the deer family and the largest land mammal in the Northeast is the Moose. A bull Moose can weigh up to twelve hundred pounds, run about forty miles an hour, and swim a little faster than two men can paddle a canoe. Moose are

Deer browse

White-tailed deer

Moose

very well-adapted to the Northern Forest, although they have an awkward, ungainly appearance at times. They are spectacular beasts. In winter, their long legs carry the bulk of their body above the snow. They survive quite well in the extreme weather of winter. Somewhat aquatic during the summer months, they are often seen feeding in lakes, ponds, and fens.

We all know that man shapes his own environment according to his needs and wants. We can sit in our climate-controlled houses and be very comfortable regardless of what is going on outside. This is very different in comparison with wildlife, all of which is shaped by the environment. The beaver, however, is the exception to this rule. The beaver is the only mammal, other than man, that creates his own habitat. This is interesting because what they do actually influences hundreds of other species of plants and animals.

Beavers, the largest rodents in North America, are strict herbivores. They feed on many species of trees, mostly hardwoods. They fell trees and eat the inner and outer bark, leaves, and twigs. They will dam up a river or stream, flooding an area, creating a pond, and then build a lodge for themselves. The trees that they most prefer are the Aspens. Aspen trees have a whitish outer layer covering much green in their bark. This can be seen with just a soft rubbing or scrape. Aspen can photosynthesize with their bark along with their leaves, enabling them to be exceptionally fast growing. However, there are some trees that the beavers avoid eating; those are the older softwood trees, which typically have thick, heavy bark. These evergreens do not like to get their feet wet. Pines need well-drained soil and die quickly after an area gets flooded by the beaver. This is where interesting things begin to happen.

It does not take very long for a population of insects to start to decompose a snag (a standing dead tree). Whenever there is a population of insects in a dead tree, very quickly a population of insectivorous birds, like woodpeckers, will be feeding on those insects.

While the woodpeckers are feeding on the insects, they open up small holes in these trees that are then used by our cavity-nesting birds like the White-breasted Nuthatch. These nuthatches usually do

Hairy Woodpecker

not build a nest on their own. They need a hole in a tree to lay their eggs in before they reproduce. So, the relationship actually can be traced from the nuthatch all the way back to the beaver.

Everything is a thread in a single fabric, a living tapestry which is all the Natural World. Intertwined and interdependent, each vibrant thread thrives in the balance of the whole. We are each a thread among the many. Rachel Carson emphasizes that nothing exists alone in nature.

> *"When we try to pick out anything by itself, we find it hitched to everything else in the universe."*
>
> —John Muir

This is the science of ecology, the study of the natural balance of relationships. Relationships between living organisms, and between these organisms and their physical environments. The more we understand these relationships, the more we see how closely connected everything is, including ourselves. We are very much a part of the whole process that is going on around us. We have an intimate relationship with this green forest that I believe is often more intimate than we think about. It happens automatically and takes place just going along on its own without us even thinking about it. It is a vital connection. These are the different threads woven into this single fabric, which is the living tapestry.

We are all aware of the importance of some of these physical relationships. We know the need for regular nourishment. We need to consume food. Most people eat two or three meals a day. However, we could survive perhaps forty days without eating. We need to take in water. Our bodies can survive possibly only three days without water. Astoundingly, we are designed so that we cannot go but a few moments without the relationship we have with the green forest. This is an interchange that takes place automatically, back and forth without conscious effort. We consume oxygen produced by the green plants and the photosynthesizing ocean-dwelling bacteria. We then give back carbon dioxide that the plants take in. This is an intimate exchange. We force air out, and the atmosphere breathes life into us. It transcends science when we see how closely connected we are with the forest on these levels. This touches on our spiritual relationship with the surrounding forest and with Nature itself.

Sugar Maple, Butter Hill Road, Chatham, New Hampshire

"Tree At My Window"
—Robert Frost

Tree at my window, window tree,
My sash is lowered when night comes on;
But let there never be curtain drawn
Between you and me.

Vague dream head lifted out of the ground,
And thing next most diffuse to cloud,
Not all your light tongues talking aloud
Could be profound.

But tree, I have seen you taken and tossed,
And if you have seen me when I slept,
You have seen me when I was taken and swept
And all but lost.

That day she put our heads together,
Fate had her imagination about her,
Your head so much concerned with outer,
Mine with inner, weather.

Sugar Maple leaf

Remember, leaves miraculously capture energy from the sun, store it in nutrients they get from the soil and the air, and then wondrously build carbohydrates. Every small leaf produces food, not only for the plant but, essentially, for everything that is alive on the planet; ourselves included. *We* are fueled with this solar energy. *We* are solar powered as a direct result of the photosynthesis that is taking place in each marvelous green leaf. Now, we see that we are also intimately exchanging our carbon dioxide for their life-giving oxygen that we need to survive.

"October's Bright Blue Weather"
—Helen Hunt Jackson

O suns and skies and clouds of June,
And flowers of June together,
Ye cannot rival for one hour
October's bright blue weather;

When loud the bumble-bee makes haste,
Belated, thriftless vagrant,
And Goldenrod is dying fast,
And lanes with grapes are fragrant;

When Gentians roll their fringes tight
To save them for the morning,
And chestnuts fall from satin burrs
Without a sound of warning;

When on the ground red apples lie
In piles like jewels shining,
And redder still on old stone walls
Are leaves of woodbine twining;

When all the lovely wayside things
Their white-winged seeds are sowing,
And in the fields, still green and fair,
Late aftermaths are growing;

When springs run low, and on the brooks,
In idle golden freighting,
Bright leaves sink noiseless in the hush
Of woods, for winter waiting;

When comrades seek sweet country haunts,
By twos and twos together,
And count like misers, hour by hour,
October's bright blue weather.

O suns and skies and flowers of June,
Count all your boasts together,
Love loveth best of all the year
October's bright blue weather.

After the fall, the second fall. The final notes of Autumn's magnum opus: the yellow brown-edged leaves of Birch and Beech, the shades of reddish browns, the tans, coppers, rusts, coffee, bronze, brunette, and russet auburn. Marcescent royalty of the late fall stand strong against the winds. An oak leaf is torn free by an abrupt draft and tumbles ground-ward, but not before one last fling on a breeze that will let it down softly to be lost in the blanket crowd. The brick reds and rusty oranges are passing and the muted tannins fade to dull. The barren Maples remain, tall, stark and waiting. The days are shorter; there is a stillness, a quiet anticipation. Across the upper elevations, the evergreen trees dominate. Even after all the deciduous trees have dropped their leaves to the ground, the evergreens hold onto theirs.

Nature has shaped trees according to their survival strategies. Deciduous trees have their branches growing up toward the sun to expose as much of the foliage as possible in order to capture as much energy as they can. They don't have to worry about the weight of the snow catching on the leaves and breaking the branches because they have already dropped those leaves. On the other hand, the evergreen trees have to be concerned about that weight because they still have their leaves. Their needle-shaped leaves will accumulate snow. Their branches must bend downward in order to shed the snow, or they will not survive. The pointed spruces and firs stand resolute in the higher elevations.

The late fall, the last stand, the last sighs of the forest as the trees breathe their last breaths before the darkest of days and the onslaught

Deciduous and Evergreen Trees; White Horse Ledge, Hale's Location, New Hampshire

Red Oak, Chatham, New Hampshire

"Everybody needs beauty as well as bread, places to play in and pray in, where nature may heal and give strength to body and soul." —John Muir

of cold, snow, and winds out of the North. Winter's long period of breathlessness to be endured, a period of thirst, without a drop of moisture to be had. A physical desert, the lakes are frozen, the rivers are crusty, and streams are often buried under ice and snow, the ground saturated with several feet of frost.

Winter comes hard and fast in Northern New England. It marches in like a bully, without regard to date or calendar, and takes for its own the last days of autumn.

Barred Owl, Chatham, New Hampshire

From "Hanover Winter Song, Dartmouth College"
—Richard Hovey 1898

For the wolf-wind is wailing at the doorways,
And the snow drifts deep along the road,
And the ice gnomes are marching from their Norways,
And the great white cold walks abroad

"...O Wind, If Winter comes, can Spring be far behind?"
—Percy B. Shelley

Winter woods

"Stopping by Woods on a Snowy Evening"
—Robert Frost

Whose woods these are I think I know.
His house is in the village though;
He will not see me stopping here
To watch his woods fill up with snow.

My little horse must think it queer
To stop without a farmhouse near
Between the woods and frozen lake
The darkest evening of the year.

He gives his harness bells a shake
To ask if there is some mistake.
The only other sound's the sweep
Of easy wind and downy flake.

The woods are lovely, dark and deep,
But I have promises to keep,
And miles to go before I sleep,
And miles to go before I sleep.

Black Bear, Chatham, New Hampshire

No matter what I do, I am never ready when winter gets here. I always have a list of chores that never get done. The four cords of wood piled out in front of the house need stacking inside before snowfall or it is twice the chore. After the snow is here, it has to be dug out and then moved inside. I never get it all done. It happens every year. I have a plan that is always interrupted and never completed. But Nature has a different way of dealing with us than she does in dealing with some of the other things under her care. We can procrastinate a little bit. We can put our chores on the back burner somewhat. But Gray Birches must have dropped those leaves to prepare themselves for winter, or they just do not survive. And, come winter, they are all ready; they have already prepared themselves.

Black Bears have to be prepared to go into a three-month deep sleep come December. They will shut down; go into this deep sleep where they will go three months without eating, without defecating; they will even give birth to one or two cubs during this sleep and nurse those cubs. A wonderful strategy for a mammal that would not be able to survive a winter in this part of the country on the type of diet that it feeds on. It is a rather rude awakening for the mother bear in the spring to find she has a couple of cubs that she did not have when she shut her eyes in December, but it works for them.

If the snow comes early, it may protect the ground dwellers with its insulating blanket: a subnivean zone created, an abode of a protected world out of reach of many predators and strong chilling winds. The snow provides an area where voles, moles, and shrews will run around under the snow and above the ground trying to avoid being caught by predators like the Red Fox who are out trying to make an honest living for themselves. However, owls have the ability to hear the scurrying of small prey even under the snow.

I think what is truly wonderful about Nature is the awareness that permeates the soul of everything. It is in the fox. It is in those mice and voles that he is chasing around under the snow. It is in the plants. And it is in all of us.

White-throated sparrow

"Be like the bird who, pausing in her flight awhile on boughs too slight, feels them give way beneath her, and yet sings, knowing she hath wings." —Victor Hugo

"God *birds* in mysterious ways, his wonders to perform."

Avian Irruptions...Regular Irregularities

Bird populations for the most part stay relatively stable over the years. Each pair of Chickadees need only have two of their eggs mature to adults over the course of the lifetime of the pair. They only need to replace themselves once, and the population will remain constant. However, Black-capped Chickadees will lay six to eight eggs every year and have been recorded to have lived up to and beyond twelve years! There is tremendous ebb and flow of individuals while populations stay fairly constant. When we see some anomaly to this balance, it can offer us other perspectives and provide a clearer vision of the dynamics of populations. Such irregular events do occur, and ornithologists call these happenings "avian irruptions."

These invasions of several species of typically northern seed-eating birds and a few species of raptors occur on a somewhat irregular basis. While most species remain on territory as permanent residents or have an annual migration, these irruptive species may migrate every two years or four years or even ten or eleven years. These irruptive species add a bit of excitement to winter bird watching and also raise several questions. What causes these irruptions? Are they associated with any regularly occurring event? Is there a relationship between one irruptive species and another? Do the food producers (plants) benefit from the emigration / immigration of these species?

These irruptive species feed on elastic food sources, the abundance of which varies from year to year. A good year of seed crop will provide nourishment for a population to increase and/or survive through the winter. The relationship between food and population size is clear. However, when after several years of growth in population, a poor crop production occurs, the question arises as to how these individuals are triggered to migrate rather than starve to death. Surprisingly, they put on fat reserves in preparation for migration (as do the annual migrants) long before the lack of food is apparent! Some ornithologists believe that it is the density of the population that the individuals sense, triggered by vocalization or repeated contact with other individuals, thus producing the migratory hormones of restlessness and preparation.

We have seen years of exceptional irruptions when several species invade in large numbers. This occurred here in the Northeast during the winter of 1997-1998 when Red and White-winged Crossbills, Common Redpolls, Evening Grosbeaks, and Pine Grosbeaks were visitors in profusion. Northern Shrike and Snowy Owl seem to irrupt about every four years, which is possibly tied to the lemming and vole cycle. Northern Goshawks have irruptions on closer to a ten-year period that seems to be associated with the cycle of Snowshoe Hare, a principal winter prey.

The mysteries of these irruptions abound, and God knows the plan. It makes for much excitement when these nomadic birds visit our area. Keep your feeders full and your binoculars close because this winter some irruptive species may show up in your yard!

Spruce Ghosts...Spirits of the Northern Forests

Up where the spruces and firs stand limb to limb, up where the winds wail with record-breaking force and snow clings to the short needles through much of the year, there are spirits that constantly wander the forest and never leave. These ghosts are always there and are only seen by those who venture into the highlands. These spirits, shaped by thousands of years of north-country weather, shaped by warm August days and frigid January nights, by rain and snow, by wind and by rime, have many names and answer to none of them. Most encounters are surprising to the unsuspecting, as these ghosts appear without announcement, without a whisper of their presence, without a word of welcome...they are just there, waiting and watching. Magical.

They must love the winter as we do because they could leave, but they stay. They welcome the spring like the rest of us in the similar position of fellow New Englanders—glad to be here and satisfied to have survived another wonderful winter here in the North and anxious for the longer days of increasing sunlight and milder temperatures. These Spruce Ghosts are busy now with the lengthening days that will eventually provide our short season of the few brief moments we call summer here in the White Mountains. With spring's arrival there is much to do now for these ghostly gray, northern beings. They are friendly spirits, apparently welcoming human visits, curious about what one might have in store for them, and bold in taking what may have been brought from that other world of humanness. They are attracted to people. They seek us out. Just the murmur of humans through the krummholz is enough to bring them in for an encounter. They move through the dense, needled forest in short flights interrupted by brief periods of perching for a quick assessment of the situation, pilfering on their minds.

Perisoreus canadensis some Linnaean-schooled birder would properly call them; others might announce them as "Camp Robbers," "Gobi birds," "Whiskey Jacks," (a corruption of their American Indian name *Wiss-ka-chion*) "Gray Jay," or by their proper common name,

Canada Jay. They are members of the Crow family and one of a genus of only three, with counterparts in northern Eurasia, the Siberian Jay (*Perisoreus infaustus*), and the Sichuan Jay (*Perisoreus internigrans*), a species endemic to China.

Although the Canada Jay often looks fairly large because its plumage is fluffed up for additional warmth most of the time, it is one of the smallest jays in the world. Sexes are similar in plumage, with the male being slightly larger in size. They have light-gray underparts, medium-gray upper-parts, and a partial black cap on the back of an otherwise white head. Juvenile birds are sooty gray all over with a slightly darker head. The vocalizations of the Canada Jay include a series of soft whistle sounds with a screeching alarm call occasionally given as a warning signal. They are silent much of the time.

A close encounter of the third kind with these boreal spirits is always an experience long remembered. An encounter I had one fall on the Webster Cliff trail brought a family of Canada Jays in for some people watching. The jays look for handouts and know that where there are people shedding their packs there is often a chance to do a little snack robbing when the opportunity presents itself. They are using a strategy that works well for them in this extreme environment with many months of limited food availability. Typically, these birds feed on insects, seeds, and fruits, and as I saw during this visit, an occasional dropped almond.

Birds that live in our northern mountains deal with an environment that produces food in abundance during one season of the year and very little during the other seasons. They employ various ways of coping with this uneven supply of sustenance. One strategy is to migrate south to areas that have more seasonal abundance during the periods of shortage in the North. The hazards of migration take their toll and are accepted by about 70 percent of our native species. A second strategy is to remain in an area and attempt to survive on the limited available resources during this time. The avoidance of high-energy consumptive activities (molting and breeding) and emphasizing strong conservation of energy (keep the thermostat set low and put on an extra blanket or a third dog on those extreme nights!) provide for ways to stretch the limited amount of available food. These species often border on the brink of starvation during the lean times, and many do not survive. A third tactic is the approach that has worked for the Canada Jay. They gather more food than is needed during times of abundance and hoard it for more difficult days in the future. This practice of hoarding is used by many northern species and has some risks of its own. Some birds may rob the caches of others, or the food may spoil and provide little nutritive value. The Canada Jays' scientific name gives away its hoarding practice with *Perisoreus* (from the Greek to "heap up") and its North American connection with *canadensis.*

Canada Jays start hoarding insects and seeds in the spring. With their unusually sticky saliva, they attach their gathered morsels to cracks and nooks in the bark of trees. They continue hoarding through the milder months and into autumn, adding mushrooms and fruit to the menu; they are known to take in an occasional mouse or toad as well as meat from leftover predator kills (including fallen ham sandwich morsels!) or other carrion. Most food is carried in their bill, but I have seen larger, more awkward-sized human food carried off with their feet. With a successful cache supply, they can start their breeding early. Canada Jay eggs have been found here in New Hampshire as early as the first of March, when it is still very much a wintry mix in the mountains.

A pair of Canada Jays found me last spring. After we watched each other for a short time, I was able to figure out where they had hidden their nest. I found it without much difficulty. It was well fastened on a horizontal leeward balsam branch about five feet above the ground. It was an artfully constructed, bulky cluster; a well-woven collection of sticks and bark, moss and grass fastened together with spider silk and insect cocoons, and lined with a few junco feathers and Moose hair. This well-insulated abode looked like a good place to raise a family in the still frozen pointed-tree forest. These nests are built by both the male and female and can take up to three weeks to complete. Four ghostly, grayish-white eggs, finely speckled with olive-buff were nestled deep inside on the mossy nest bottom. They were just over an inch in length, and it was difficult to imagine that each contained a complete set of instructions for a soon-to-be-new Spruce Ghost! This would be the only brood of the year for this monogamous pair, and they would watch over the nest for over a month. The female does the incubation and after sixteen to eighteen days, the altricial young (immobile, naked, eyes closed) will break out of the shells. Over the next two weeks, they will quickly grow to adult size and leave the nest. Both parents will continue to feed them for another four or five weeks. Then something interesting happens. The fledglings begin to clash with one another, and after about ten days, one dominant bird has established itself. This bird will accompany the parents for at least the next year, foraging and hoarding with the parents and receiving the protection of this small flock. It is estimated that eighty percent of the remaining young do not survive this first, now rapidly approaching winter.

Just a passing encounter with these Spruce Ghosts is enough to raise one's perspective and provide a new insight into the workings of the northern forests. A glimpse of a spirit, an apparition that is here and then gone, a taste of another world much different from our own. Keep your eyes open and your head up when traveling the North Woods, and you too may be touched by the friendly Spruce Ghosts of these White Mountains.

Adapted from "Christmas Bells"
—Henry Wadsworth Longfellow

I heard the bells on Christmas day
Their old familiar carols play
And wild and sweet their songs repeat
Of peace on Earth good will to men

And in despair I bowed my head
There is no peace on Earth I said
For hate is strong and mocks the song
Of peace on Earth, good will to men

Then pealed the bells more loud and deep
God is not dead, nor does he sleep
The wrong shall fail, the right prevail
With peace on Earth, good will to men

And ringing singing on its way
The world revolved from night to day
A voice, a chime, a chant sublime
Of peace on Earth, good will to men

Open your heart to hear them
Peace on Earth, good will to men

"Through Him all things came to be, not one thing has its being but through Him. All that came to be has life in him and that life is the light of all mankind, a light that shines in the dark, a light that darkness cannot overpower."

—John 1:3-5

"And Heaven and Nature Sing"

—Joy to the World

And "...ringing, singing on its way, the world revolved from night to day." Earth's dance around the sun proceeds from darkness to increasing light, and the seasons' song plays on with subtle daily changes to the melody. Nighttime narrows and day lengthens, snowmelt trickles into rivulets, buds erupt, and the "flasks of heaven" tilt out the showers of spring. Bird lovers watch for returning travelers and document their homecoming to feeder, field, or forest.

Why do our hearts lift when we hear the Tufted Titmouse begin to sing? Why do our spirits rise when we first hear the notes of the Chickadee's "spring song"? Perhaps it is because this is the voice of God's faithfulness, heralding the promise of more glorious days to come. No matter how long, dark, and cold winter has been, we can be certain that spring will come. It is with grateful hearts that we welcome this testament of God's loving care.

Maple sugaring
"A sap run is the sweet goodbye of winter. It is the fruit of the equal marriage of the sun and frost." —John Burroughs

Excerpt from "Two Tramps in Mud Time"
—Robert Frost

The sun was warm but the wind was chill.
You know how it is with an April day
When the sun is out and the wind is still,
You're one month on in the middle of May.
But if you so much as dare to speak,
A cloud comes over the sunlit arch,
A wind comes off a frozen peak,
And you're two months back in the middle of March.

"It was one of those March days when the sun shines hot and the wind blows cold; when it is summer in the light, and winter in the shade."

—Charles Dickens

We all know that eventually the long winter will come to an end. And suddenly the forest just comes alive with spring. The flowers will start to blossom, the migrants return singing, and all become completely involved in their complex spring nuptials. It is an exciting time, and before we know it, in the blink of an eye, Autumn will come creeping up under the guise of bright days and warm temperatures. Then when our guard is down, it is here, and the trees are no longer vibrating green, and we realize summer is gone. The seasons seem to go by just about that fast. Don't miss their passing!

"I wandered lonely as a Cloud"
—William Wordsworth

I wandered lonely as a Cloud
That floats on high o'er Vales and Hills,
When all at once I saw a crowd,
A host of golden Daffodils;
Beside the Lake, beneath the trees,
Fluttering and dancing in the breeze.
Continuous as the stars that shine
And twinkle on the Milky Way,
They stretched in never-ending line
Along the margin of a bay:
Ten thousand saw I at a glance,
Tossing their heads in sprightly dance.
The waves beside them danced, but they
Out-did the sparkling waves in glee: —
A Poet could not but be gay
In such a jocund company:
I gazed—and gazed—but little thought
What wealth the shew to me had brought:
For oft when on my couch I lie
In vacant or in pensive mood,
They flash upon that inward eye
Which is the bliss of solitude,
And then my heart with pleasure fills,
And dances with the Daffodils.

Lupine, Crawford Notch, New Hampshire

Excerpt from "The Vision of Sir Launfal"
—James Russell Lowell

'Tis heaven alone that is given away,
'Tis only God may be had for the asking;
No price is set on the lavish summer;
June may be had by the poorest comer.

And what is so rare as a day in June?
Then, if ever, come perfect days;
Then Heaven tries the Earth if it be in tune,
And over it softly her warm ear lays:
Whether we look, or whether we listen,
We hear life murmur, or see it glisten;

Every clod feels a stir of might,
    An instinct within it that reaches and towers,
And, groping blindly above it for light,
    Climbs to a soul in grass and flowers;
The flush of life may well be seen
    Thrilling back over hills and valleys;
The cowslip startles in meadows green,
    The buttercup catches the sun in its chalice,
And there's never a leaf nor a blade too mean
    To be some happy creature's palace;
The little bird sits at his door in the sun,
    Atilt like a blossom among the leaves,
And lets his illumined being o'errun
    With the deluge of summer it receives;
His mate feels the eggs beneath her wings,
And the heart in her dumb breast flutters and sings;
He sings to the wide world, and she to her nest, —
In the nice ear of Nature which song is the best?

Now is the high-tide of the year,
    And whatever of life hath ebbed away
Comes flooding back with a ripply cheer,
    Into every bare inlet and creek and bay;
Now the heart is so full that a drop over-fills it,
We are happy now because God wills it;
No matter how barren the past may have been,
'Tis enough for us now that the leaves are green;
We sit in the warm shade and feel right well
How the sap creeps up and the blossoms swell;
We may shut our eyes, but we cannot help knowing
That skies are clear and grass is growing;
The breeze comes whispering in our ear,
That dandelions are blossoming near,
    That maize has sprouted, that streams are flowing,
That the river is bluer than the sky,

That the robin is plastering his house hard by;
And if the breeze kept the good news back,
For other couriers we should not lack;
    We could guess it all by yon heifer's lowing, —
And hark! how clear bold chanticleer,
Warmed with the new wine of the year,
    Tells all in his lusty crowing!

"Summer in the South"
—Paul Laurence Dunbar

The oriole sings in the greening grove
As if he were half-way waiting,
The rosebuds peep from their hoods of green,
Timid, and hesitating.
The rain comes down in a torrent sweep
And the nights smell warm and piney,
The garden thrives, but the tender shoots
Are yellow-green and tiny.
Then a flash of sun on a waiting hill,
Streams laugh that erst were quiet,
The sky smiles down with a dazzling blue
And the woods run mad with riot.

Bird Listing—Field Exercise #3

Making a list and checking it twice.

I have been a maker of lists for as long as I can remember. I make a new "to-do list" while sipping my first cup of coffee each morning. Overlooking the pond and watching the first arrivals at the feeders, I bullet what I have planned for myself that day. On my laptop, I have a master to-do list with many accomplishments yet unattained, which I keep updated in a program called ToDo! I tweak it repeatedly in an attempt to make myself think that I have some control over my life, adding a thought, a task, or an idea for later ruminating when time or place allows. I have taken something beyond reach at that moment, gotten it down on paper (or keyboard), and given it some shape and substance.

Early in the calendar year is a time for new goals, new beginnings, and new lists. Many bird watchers keep a "Life List." This is a record of the first encounter with a species of bird, a running register of every species they have ever seen in their life. Each entry would typically include the species seen, the date, the location, and any additional notes one may wish to record. In addition to a journal entry, many birders use a checklist to tick off the species for a quick reference to their life tally of birds. Most field guides include a checklist. The quest for additional entries often leads to excursions to new places, both locally and globally, in search of more birds for the list. It is a way to *collect* the bird and remember the encounter. Looking back over the years, a simple journal entry is enough to bring back the memories for study or reminiscing. It also provides a method for learning and becoming a more proficient observer. Computer programs make the list-keeping even more productive and useful. This is not just some neurotic behavior of one infected with the birding virus; it is a valuable tool. The mobility of birds makes them a difficult target for study, but there is much joy in discovering the mysteries of their ways. Ornithologists need information from many sources, and observant amateur bird watchers provide important data that researchers can use in their studies.

A Life List often leads to the keeping of additional bird lists. Some birders keep a "Yard List" of all the birds they see in the vicinity of their home and feeders. Some will keep a separate "State List" for each new species encountered in a particular state. I have a close friend who even keeps a "Media List" of all the birds he sees or hears in movies or on TV (avian vocalizations heard in the background of a scene often indicate species that, in the real world, never visit that particular locale!). Some birders even keep a "Wish List" of birds they hope to see!

Exercising the lists help shape the science and art of bird watching. One of my favorite and most useful lists is a "Year List" of the birds that I have seen from January 1st through December 31st of each year. Each entry elevates the sighting to a heightened level: the first Junco of the year, the first Tree Sparrow of the winter, the first returning Red-winged Blackbird announcing that spring is not far behind! For some reason we are attracted to superlatives, and "Year Lists" feed that thirst in an interesting way. As with so much of what we do, the actual fruit of our actions is often on a different level than the process. The keeping of a list can be very much its own accomplishment that goes beyond tallying species, as it quietly focuses one's attention while developing some strength in observing. Listers will soon feel the pulse of the avian rhythms as it changes with the length of day.

I have already added the usual contingent from my feeders and am watchful for any new visitors that will be passing through in the days ahead. As the year proceeds, I find myself getting back to old familiar haunts to see the usual birds I expect to find in attendance. Recently, I made a trek over to Portland Head Light. Fort Williams Park in the winter is one of my favorite places, although I doubt I would have taken the time unless there were some specific goal other than a walk along the bitter January coast of Maine. I had several species of seabirds that were not yet on my "Year List" to *capture* and record! When I don't find a Canada Warbler at my favorite beaver bog in early May, it is like missing an old friend, and the visit provides some information on a late or early migration, or possibly some change in the habitat there. Maybe I will find something new that has not been recorded in years past, more fodder for speculation.

If you have not started your Life List, make your first entry today. If you already have a Life List, then start your "Year List" for this year and see just how many entries you have by the end of December. Add a new feeder to the yard and see how fast the lists grow. Take a walk on a familiar path and add a few entries. Visit someplace new and give some Chickadees an opportunity to get *you* on their life lists.

Pine River, Ossipee, New Hampshire

"Rivers flow not past us but through us; tingling, vibrating, exciting every cell and fiber in our bodies making them sing and glide." —John Muir

Pine River Treasure

I recall only bits and pieces of a long-ago summer adventure with my siblings. However, those bits and pieces represent a formative experience that I can still *feel* today.

As one of the younger siblings, I was not responsible for any of the planning or preparation. All that was required of me was to refrain from unreasonable complaints when the going got tough, and from telling on any of my perhaps overzealous or cantankerous fellow travelers. But I was not merely along for the ride; I was a true participant and brought along my full imagination and, gloriously, no expectations of how this adventure was *supposed* to unfold.

My brother Paul was certain we would find gold along the Pine River in Effingham/Ossipee. one of the few New Hampshire rivers that flow north (actually northwest). We put in to the river at a spot not far from the Bungalow in Effingham; two crafts: my grandfather's small, flat-bottomed rowboat and Paul's Sailfish minus centerboard and sail. Our final destination was the river's mouth in Ossipee Lake. Both places were familiar to me, but it wasn't long before we entered a totally unknown realm. We pushed off from the bank with loud, excited laughter, but we were soon hushed by the river's own sounds.

The branches hung low on either side of the narrow river and would occasionally pat us on the head as we passed beneath. As light danced with shadow, it felt as though we were in another time. We moved along so slowly that I felt a slowing in myself, a stillness, yet there was much activity all around. The bird calls were mostly unfamiliar, and an unknown animal occasionally splashed in or out of the water out of sight up ahead or behind somewhere. When the river twisted back on itself, we would lose sight of the front boat and then we would hear them, unseen, beside us. It was all so eerie, strange, and beautiful.

There was an assortment of wildlife: insects, turtles, Wood Ducks, and Mergansers, a Barred Owl, and an occasional Mink slipping quickly out of sight; some creatures easily recognized, some unknown.

The river flowed into a somewhat open area and, in full-throated amazement, I spotted a Pterodactyl flying low overhead with huge outspread wings, pointed beak and long legs trailing behind. I was quickly laughed to silence and told it was a "Great Blue" probably headed to the Heath. It was still an awesome sight.

Great Blue Heron

Gold was spotted several times, glinting beautifully in shimmering sunlight on the river bottom. We would reach down through the shallow water, only to bring an unassuming rock to the surface. The river's meandering ways and the need, a few times, to lift the boats over downed logs turned what was supposed to be a few hours into a day-long expedition. When we saw the first sign of civilization, an overpass, it was decided we would call it a day.

So the trip's objective, to find gold, was not achieved. And we never made it to our planned destination, Ossipee Lake. But none of us was the least bit disappointed in our voyage. As with all travel, the gem is the journey itself. We each came away with lasting treasure.

Herring Gull

The real voyage of discovery consists not in seeking new lands but seeing with new eyes." —Marcel Proust

Chapter Six

Travel—Passage to Another Place

Like migrating land and seabirds or the albatross forever on the wing, we too feel that urge to depart. Coming at various times and in varying degrees, that yearning to go, to venture forth, to risk the journey is simply an inherent part of who we are.

The *adventure* depends not on length of time or distance traveled, but more importantly, on how wide-awake the traveler is. All travel involves travail, some trouble or difficulty, an obstacle to be overcome. In whatever guise this trouble presents, it is important to keep in mind that the obstacle to be overcome is actually our own Self wanting to be in control of this adventure, wanting to manipulate the details in order to fit with our own expectations. However, true travel experience is to let go of our expectations and let the adventure unfold as it will, revealing wonders. It is interesting that the word "travail" has been used in reference to childbirth: first the struggle, the labor, and then the deliverance of new (renewed) life. Think of your travel as a quest, an adventurous expedition to find something of value.

Then there is the great "Going Home." We all have a heartfelt longing for home. To be "Homeward Bound," to be recalled to a welcome place of familiarity and comfort. It is an old truism, yet still powerful, Home is *wherever* the Heart is. Our internal compass is always set to Home.

Monarch Butterfly

As I write this, we are in the early days of September. A stunning *lepidoptera* floats into my line of vision and then, just as suddenly, sails off in a different direction. This visit from the butterfly world, a member of the "super generation," reminds me that the great *going home* of the Monarchs of North America has begun. These majestic creatures, weighing less than a gram, will travel fifty to a hundred miles a day, and their journey may be as long as three thousand miles back to a fir forest in Mexico. The average Monarch's lifespan is only a couple of months, and it takes several generations of Monarchs to make the journey from Mexico all the way up to New England and Canada. But the last generation, the "super generation" who live up to eight months, will make it all the way *back home* to Mexico; amazingly *back* to a place they have never *physically* been before. Next spring, it is this "super generation" that will fly the first leg of the northward migration; mating, laying their eggs, and dying along the way. And in doing so, they will have passed on to their grandchildren's grandchildren the way home. It gives me pause to think about what our ancestors may have left with us. *Home* is not only physical or emotional, it is also spiritual. We are being called home, to a home we do not consciously remember. We know the way. Placed within each of us is a powerful force, a spiritual longing. All of Nature, within and without, is continually speaking to us in a myriad of ways; we just have to listen.

> *"...Before I was born the* Lord *called me;*
> *from my mother's womb he has spoken my name..."*
>
> —Isaiah 49:1

> *"You have made known to me the paths of life; you will fill me with joy in your presence."*
>
> —Acts 2:8

There are many modes of travel, and any path will take you.

When you unmoor your little boat and set sail for another place, whether it be another town or another country—close to home or halfway around the globe—you let go of your routines and leave behind all that is commonplace to you. You look with fresh eyes at your novel surroundings. You see as with the eyes of a child—with innocence, not with preconceptions or jaded vision. There is great value in being in this world, yet set down in a new environment ("a stranger in a strange land"); free of the distractions, the responsibilities, and the preoccupations of being *home* in the ultra-familiar where we may be blind and deaf to that which we are so very accustomed. An experience like this gives us new perspective—a change in perception that alters us, increasing our sense of awareness of our world and ourselves.

Travel can be an extremely enriching experience and beneficial to your well-being. You return home changed and see the familiar with new sight. However, as John Burroughs, the well-renowned nineteenth-century naturalist, said, *"Do not despise your own place and time...The lure of the distant and the difficult is deceptive. The great opportunity is where you are."*

You do not have to climb Kilimanjaro or Everest or cross an ocean to parts unknown in order to seek and find new experiences, new insights, or new ways of seeing your world. Your own neighborhood, your own backyard is full of wondrous things that Nature is calling you to appreciate. You only need to learn to *see* what is there.

For example, here in the White Mountains of New Hampshire, folks have a natural wonder in their neighborhood—Mt. Washington. It is constantly photographed, frequently the subject of artists' works, and seen daily by the many who live in these parts. Unfortunately, it is often seen only as another pretty picture-postcard sight. Many folks have never seen beyond—to its history, its wonders, and its magic. They have not yet learned to see the treasure that it is.

Let's take a closer look at Mt. Washington and the White Mountains of Northern New England.

These ancient Appalachians, believed by many to be the oldest mountains in the world, have stood here for over four hundred million years. Some geologists believe that when they were young, they were the highest mountains in the world—perhaps even higher than the Himalayas are today. They have been shaped and worn by ice age upon ice age, the most recent being the Wisconsin Glacier which only receded ten to two thousand years ago.

Mt. Washington Tip Top House

Mt. Washington is not only the highest peak in the White Mountains, it is the highest peak in the entire Northeast. It stands 6,288 feet above sea level. That may not sound very high to many folks, but small though it may be, it has the worst weather that has been recorded anywhere at any elevation in the world. A clear indication of this is the fact that the tree line (the varying elevation at which tree growth is no longer typical) comes in on Mt.

Washington at about five thousand feet. The tree line in the Western Rockies comes in at twice that elevation, ten thousand to eleven thousand feet, indicating that here we have a much harsher climate at a much lower elevation.

These White Mountains stand at the crossroads of many weather systems that sweep across their summits. The highest wind ever recorded on the planet by man was recorded on the summit of Mt. Washington on April 12, 1934–231 miles per hour. Winter conditions can exist there at any time of the year. This presents a severe problem for hikers who are not used to the type of climate they may encounter at high elevations here in the Northeast. When they set out on a hike, it may be a beautiful, calm, and sunny day. Then, with little or no warning, the weather may change drastically, turning into arctic conditions. Unfortunately, an average of two lives are lost every year, most of them during July and August.

Mt. Washington Weather Tower

Remarkably, there are buildings located on the summit of Mt. Washington: radio and television transmitters, communication antennas, and a weather observatory that is constantly monitoring present weather conditions and issuing both local predictions and contributing to national forecasts. People live and work there every day, year-round. This fact is a testament to the ability of humans to create and shape their own environment, keeping themselves warm and safe, rather than being shaped by the environment the way wildlife is.

The American Indians called the Mountain, *Agiocochook*. This has been translated several ways: Home of the Great Spirit, Place of the Spirit of the Forest, Place of the Storm Spirit. They did not climb to the summit because they believed it was the dwelling place of the Great Spirit.

Today, the summit may be reached by three different ways:

- By foot—There are a variety of hiking trails with varying degrees of difficulty.
- By a cog railway—The first mountain-climbing cog railway in the world, it is three miles long, scales the western slope, and has been called, "The little engine that could." The Cog's first trip to the summit was July 3, 1869.
- By an auto road that winds almost eight miles up the eastern slope of the Mountain; it was completed in August 1861 as a horse and carriage road.

For every thousand feet gained in elevation here in the Northeast, there are climate changes comparable to a northerly latitude increase of about 250 miles. For instance, in a few hours, you can drive from the Atlantic coast beginning at Portsmouth, New Hampshire, or Portland, Maine, to the highest peak in the White Mountains. As you journey, you will see changes in the forest as though you had remained at sea level and traveled north about fifteen hundred miles, putting yourself just within the Arctic Circle.

I have been north to the Arctic, and I have also visited it often above tree line here in the White Mountains. We have the same forces at work. Some plants and animals of these areas of high elevation in Northern New Hampshire are the same species we find in

Mt. Washington Western Slope and Cog Railway

the Arctic. The American Pipit (*Anthus rubescens*), a songbird that nests in both Arctic tundra and alpine meadows, also nests in the alpine zone of Mt. Washington. I saw my first American Pipit on the "Rock Pile" in 1988. A male making its spectacular mating display over the rocks and sedges of the cloud-swept summit drew *my* attention, even if not the attention of a suitable mate. A nest was found a few years later confirming this southernmost breeding location in the East. This population now seems to be stable with ten to twenty pairs tucked into the cushion plants and larger sharp-angled rocks above tree line. This habitat is shaped by the same arctic environmental forces as one would find fifteen hundred miles north…little difference except for latitude. The Blackpoll Warbler (*Setophaga striata*) is found in the evergreens of the Mountain in one of their most southern nesting populations. Most of this species raise their young in the boreal forests of northern Canada. This southern nesting habitat provides for a shorter flight for this long-distance migrating species that winters in the Caribbean and northern South America. A few other birds that typically nest further north opt for this relatively high-elevation habitat. Many plants work the same strategy on the Mountain. Northern species like Alpine Azalea (*Loiseleuria procumbens*) and Diapensia (*Diapensia lapponica*) are common above tree line, adding to the arctic tundra-like conditions. A short season of rapid bloom and shutdown seems to work for these ground-hugging plants that stay low and out of the wind and are exposed to much sunlight during the longest days of June and July. Survival of the *shortest* seems to be the rule when the trees give way to the harsh environment above five thousand feet. Robbin's Cinquefoil, the dwarf mountain cinquefoil (*Potentilla robbinsiana*) is endemic to the White Mountains and is found

Diapensia, Mt. Washington

only on Mt. Washington and on the Franconia Ridge just to the west. This tiny perennial is a member of the rose family and, with almost stemless yellow blossoms, stays close to the ground and out of harm's way from some of the fiercest winds and weather in the world. It is a treasure of this unusual Mt. Washington ecosystem.

Mt. Washington is located halfway between the equator and the North Pole. Traveling up the mountain, we see a mixture of flora and fauna neither as limited in number as those in the Arctic, nor as diverse as those on the equator. As we travel beyond the forest toward the summit, we pass through the krummholz forest of spruce and fir, gnarled and crippled by the forces of the North.

One of the *newest* birds to be carved out of tricky and complex taxonomy, breeds here in this stunted treescape of the Northeast. Once considered a subspecies of the Gray-cheeked Thrush (*Catharus minimus*), Bicknell's Thrush (*Catharus bicknelli*) was elevated to its own species in 1995. This thrush can only be found nesting at elevations above three thousand feet in the northeastern forests (and at lower elevations in higher latitudes in similarly stunted spruce and fir coastal forests of New Brunswick, Canada), another specialized occupant of this rich and fascinating environment of Mt. Washington.

Undercast Mt. Washington

Visiting the summit of Mt. Washington is always exciting and magical. The summit is in the clouds sixty percent of the time. These mountains create their own weather. Sometimes, in the valleys below, it can be *overcast* and raining. However, as you travel up the Mountain, you may pass through the clouds into a dazzlingly bright and sunny day. As you stroll on the summit, you can look down on the eerily beautiful *undercast* of clouds that are raining on the valleys below. If the surrounding summits are emerging out of the clouds all around you, they may resemble strange turrets of ancient castles in a magical kingdom. Then you may think you know how Jack felt when he climbed the beanstalk, broke through the clouds, and saw the giant's castle for the first time. On a very clear day you can see into five states, Canada, and the Atlantic Ocean. Mt. Washington is indeed a wondrous place and brings joy to those who know it well enough to appreciate its subtle enchantment.

Mt. Washington Summit

Some of my friends who work at the summit of Mt. Washington tell me that there are only two seasons up there—winter and the fourth of July! But that is not the truth. I took this photo several years ago at the summit—on the fourth of July.

Remember, everywhere, in everyone's backyard or neighborhood, there are wonders and magical places like Mt. Washington waiting to be experienced. No matter where you are, Nature is there, whether on a mountain top, deep in the woods, in a suburban yard, or a city park. It could be as small and as ordinary in appearance as a clump of trees or a field of wildflowers, in your own yard or just down the street. We simply need to turn our attention and find ways to be out among them.

> *"I go to nature to be soothed and healed, and to have my senses put in order."*
>
> —John Burroughs

Fenway Park, Boston, Massachusetts

Birding at Fenway

Bill "Spaceman" Lee on Fenway Park: *"I couldn't find the park, and when I found it, I said, 'This not a park, this is a factory.' And then you walk through the gates, and you come through that little tunnel and then all of a sudden you see the green of the seats, the green of the wall, the green of the field and the little dirt cut-out and the proximity of the foul line to the seats, the closeness of the bullpens to the crowd, and it's like you go down all of a sudden on one knee and you bless yourself, and think, 'Thank God for making me a ballplayer, 'cause this is heaven.'"*

Summers ago, driving Route 16, Ossipee, cumulus fluffs forming in a deep-blue sky; the familiar smell of the pines and Sweetfern surrounding Ossipee Lake was heavy in the humid air of early morning, as I breezed south on my way *home*. I had moved from the North Shore of Boston to North Conway, New Hampshire, the year the Red Sox won the 1967 American League Pennant. Now, many years later, the route to Boston is a familiar one with time to ponder days ahead and days behind. Heading to a place I used to call home; heading to Boston and a place that I had spent many an afternoon. Heading now for a Saturday afternoon battle between the Red Sox and the Yankees; to a place that always feels like home…Fenway Park.

Many years ago, a friend (despite being a Yankee fan) had told me about the birds he had seen at Fenway. I wanted to see just how the birding was these days, now that the Sox were back in contention. It was a time of Yankees domination then, and I wondered what avian activity had changed since the Sox had broken "the curse."

An opportunity for an afternoon game delayed for a national TV broadcast made for even better timing; late afternoon into early evening. Along with some nostalgia, I brought the expectations of seeing the usual avian suspects. I had a few surprises in store.

Earlier I had packed my binocs and rain gear for an afternoon in the bleachers. I motored south through the greens of Maples and Birches, a tossed salad of the waning verdant summer. Rochester, Dover, Portsmouth and the big right turn and down the homestretch to Boston.

Yawkey Way, Fenway Park, Boston, Massachusetts

Fenway Park is cradled in wetlands, the Back Bay Fens. A fen is a freshwater marsh, and Boston's fens are made by the Muddy River seeping through and slowly making its way on into the Charles and eventually out into Boston Harbor. A feng shui of magical focused energy made a perfect arena for the game of baseball.

Walking up to the Park is like approaching a shrine. The festivities of Yawkey Way—now cut off from traffic and filled with smoking sausages, pizza, beer, balloons and screaming program-barkers—resembles a summer Fryeburg Fair. The energy overflows from the throng of fans in high spirits with game time approaching.

It was early afternoon and, once one walks through the gate, all watches slow to an immeasurable ticking. Baseball is timeless, one of the few games not controlled by the clock until recent years. The brick and steel of Fenway Park hold true to that timelessness. The game's purpose is to be *safe* and to get *home*, so I felt as if I were winning even before the first pitch.

My dad took me to my first game in the early sixties, and I was jolted into a different reality, like something out of Carlos Castaneda. It was too small. It was not the giant field that I had seen so often on TV. But it was clear and crisp and in color! Was this really it, or just some other joke my Old Man was playing on me? It was magic. My first memory of falling in love. It was real, and I fell deeply that day at first sight from the alleyway of the grandstands along the first-base line.

The dayglow grass, the verdant Monster towering over left field, the unceasing chatter of the crowd; the game stays the same, only the players, the price of beer, and the birds seem to change. The enchantment is intoxicating.

Mourning Doves celebrating the start of the game, an abundance of popcorn, a feast for the feathered, as well as the fans. These doves get their name from the mournful coos they make, and today I'm convinced it is tied to the Red Sox past. They are having a time of it this afternoon; cruising in tandem with aerial precision beyond that of the Blue Angels; swooping around, over and under the framework of a ballpark that is unique among all the stadiums across the country.

A couple of Rock Pigeons, several House Sparrows and a few Eurasian Starlings; all British connections from the 1890s. These European species were released here on the East Coast back when fans were watching the Boston Beaneaters and the Boston Pilgrims bat the ball around and long before the 1912 opening of Fenway Park.

The bleachers—the cheap seats, no complaints from me—are my favorite place to experience the game and best for watching the afternoon avian activity. Historically, these birds would have been sipping water in the fen; now the puddles in the concrete depressions of Row 22 will have to do. A satisfying quench in this blistering summer sun; rain last night and possibly more today. A gulp of draft lager works equally well for me.

The same pair of "MoDo"s (Mourning Doves), one over and one through the framework of the Budweiser sign over the covered right field grandstand, wing their way across center field. Both birds settle on the cap of the left field giant forty-foot Coke bottle, the thirst quencher of the Green Monster. Loudspeakers greet the 35,000-plus anxious fans: "Welcome to Fenway Park, the most beloved ballpark in America!" Deafening cheers rise from the stands, and we take a step closer to the game.

A bright overcast. The national anthem and all the birds are up. A Common Grackle flies low over the Yankee bullpen and up across the fans of Section 44 and out of the park with "the rockets' red glare," like a home run over the Ford sign in the right field bleachers beyond anyone's reach.

A cluster of Yankee fans huddle six rows down in front of me. Opposing fans come in on the Rock Pigeon level if you are a bird snob; common, gregarious, introduced from away. Yankees are on the board with an early run. Sox tie it up in the third.

The bleachers used to be filled with old men and a few truant kids who had negotiated the MTA of bus and rail at the cost of a dime, transfers, and a missed afternoon of sixth grade. Any kid tall enough to ride could make it into the city in a matter of minutes. Now I am the old guy, and there are very few kids. Now mostly women fill the bleachers: summer-clad, hot, and somewhat sultry (like the weather), many of them wearing uniform tops with their favorite player's name across the back shoulders. It used to be only the players who wore the uniforms.

The bleacher gang is already a bit wild, mob mentality loosely controlled, simmering on the brink of chaos. The Yankee fans are subdued. The experience is surreal, all watching millionaires playing a game. It is a bizarre happening.

Top of the fourth, high, directly over the pitcher's mound, the heftiest of our Buteos, an adult Red-tailed Hawk is riding the ocean breeze out of the east. It takes only an occasional flap to shift his view of the happenings below. He makes a few minor adjustments to his wing tips and rusty-red tail. In a casual rhythm, he wings his way up to the back of the light array on the first-base side. He ruffles his feathers and settles in for a three-inning stay. Later, he makes a flight over the field. No fans appear to take any interest. He returns to his perch after his seventh-inning stretch and acts like a season-ticket holder in a familiar viewing spot. Fans are much more interested in Ben Affleck in his usual season perch beside the Red Sox dugout.

Two Herring Gulls and one Great Black-back Gull are in flight outside the gate over Landsdown Street. They shift with the breeze and now drift over center field, riding high on the east wind that brings a refreshing coolness off the harbor and the smell of salt air and memories of growing up on the North Shore—bottom of the Fourth.

A fly-over Mallard is silhouetted in the darkening sky. Lights are on at five-of-five under gray storm clouds. Rain at two minutes before five; there's a rain delay, and the birds and ball players settle down. Steady rain, bright in the west now and the sun struggling to shine again. All is comfortable in Section 38 with the Sox out in front and, with the foresight of packing, an umbrella in one hand and a full beer clenched in the other—five to five.

Top of the seventh, a Yankee's bat connects, sending the ball for a ride over the fence and into the right field grandstands. The Yankee fans are on their feet, but the lead is short-lived. Bottom of the seventh, and the Sox load the bases with no outs. They continue to rap the ball around some and by the end of the inning, the Sox are up ten to six. Top of the Eighth, the Red-tail makes a brief circle of the Park and disappears out beyond the lights. Yankees' bats are hushed—out in order. The birds are quiet too.

A Black-crowned Night Heron flyover in the bottom of the Eighth, heading toward the Charles. The Sox are on top, and the crowd is chanting Neil Diamond's "Sweet Caroline"—*"good times never seemed so good"*—taunting the boys from the Bronx. I am quiet and prefer to count the birds after hatching rather than still in the egg, a lesson learned from my dad who had four coronaries before he died, three of them directly attributed to constant Red Sox disappointments.

Suddenly visible out of the darkness of the left field grandstands and into the lights, wings the fastest animal in the world, a Peregrine

Falcon, across center field on a straight course between the right field Dunkin' Donuts' sign and the Budweiser letters. He is gone as quickly as he came. Falconers call this genus of birds "Longwings." They row through the atmosphere with deep, strong thrusts that make them a formidable predator capable of hitting speeds of 230 mph in powered dives in pursuit of prey—king of beers, king of birds—now casually cruising closer to twenty miles an hour, a *walk* in the Park. They are probably nesting on one of the tall, cliff-like buildings nearby and keeping the Rock Pigeon population stable. There's not a pigeon in sight. The birds were quiet in the wake of the falcon and quiet, too, continued the Yankees' bats and fans.

Ninth inning and several Ring-billed Gulls move through the high light overhead, possibly awaiting the spoils of the stands. A winning day at Fenway all around with the Red Sox on top eleven to six, almost as many Sox runs as birds, with a bird species for each Sox run plus one for good luck!

Wherever you are, Nature is! Miracles exist whatever the environs. Wherever you live, Nature has marvels, adventures, and insights just waiting to be realized. Nature Absorption is the key that opens the door!

We are all travelers here on Earth, which is itself a traveler in the solar system, on a voyage through our Milky Way Galaxy, all proceeding on our way in the cosmos. There are life-changing adventures to be had.

Hurricane Mt. Road, Chatham, New Hampshire

"It's your road, and yours alone.
Others may walk it with you,
but no one can walk it for you." —Rumi

Sugar Maple, Butter Hill Road, Chatham, New Hampshire

"I took a walk in the woods and came out taller than the trees."
—Henry David Thoreau

"I went into the woods because I wished to live deliberately, to front only the essential facts of life, and see if I could learn what it had to teach, and not, when I came to die, discovered that I had not lived."

—Henry David Thoreau

"Beyond the Gate"
—J.K.L.

Venture out beyond the gate,
Your walking stick and lantern take.
It's not an errand, not a chore,
Just simply going out the door.

The hills are calling out to you,
And only you can answer.

Ramble beside the murmuring brooks,
The whispering trees and laughing rooks.
Listen deeply, as this path you stroll;
God's gentle voice you will always know,
Heard with heart, understood with soul.

Walk on,
For what you seek awaits beyond,
Just up ahead.
Walk on,
Walk on.

Stride freely,
Each step on holy ground,
A sanctuary in the present, found.

Graylag Geese, Reykjavik, Iceland

An early morning walk is a blessing for the whole day." —Henry David Thoreau

Wayfaring—Traveling by Foot

"May you walk gently through the world and know its beauty all the days of your life."

—Apache Blessing

"In every walk with nature, one receives far more than he seeks."

—John Muir

A walk is a wonderful (wonder-filled) activity, whether shared or solitary, an experience as varied as its many names: stroll, stride, saunter, amble, hike, meander, tramp, wander, and so forth.

There is freedom in a stride. The physical freedom of roaming, wandering; and the freedom of mind, allowing free-flowing thoughts and feelings, where your thoughts are freely open to *You*. That is why often during a walk, or soon afterward, a solution to some conundrum or a different outlook will present itself.

Walking is a gesture, a touching, a way to connect the Earth, your physical body, and your spirit mind. There is a rhythm in walking, both external and internal movement; the outward movement of the feet and legs calms and quiets the inner self (mind). Feel your heart's beating within you and your increased breath; feel each step placed upon the Earth. Unlike running or jogging, in walking there is always one foot on the ground. Walking is unpretentious, simple, *down-to-Earth*.

Direct contact of bare feet to the Earth has additional benefits as explained by Clint Ober in his concept of "Earthing." Humans have walked and slept on this planet in direct contact with the Earth for thousands of years. Until fairly recent years, when the advent of rubber soles on our shoes served to insulate us from the Earth, we were actually in contact with the ground itself. We are not only chemically regulated, but we have our own electrical current and are very much a conductive part of the planet. When we touch the ground, Earth energy is transferred that has a natural healing element that restores an ageless link to Nature…to Mother Earth.

We directly connect and share electrons that can influence our health, our sleep, and our appearance. Accordingly, Earthing can quickly reconnect one with the life-supporting energy of the Earth and can be measured with a simple electrical meter.

> *"All life is sacred and all creation related. What we do affects the whole universe. So let us walk in balance with Mother Earth and all her peoples."*
>
> —Smiling Bear, American Indian

Untether yourself from the devices that compel you to be always elsewhere, constantly drawn away, missing, and never really here. Step away, release yourself from those bonds, and step out into the heart of Nature. "The hills are calling out to you, and only you can answer."

Be a "walker, errant," a traveler in search of adventure. It doesn't matter whether the journey has a destination or not, or whether you walk familiar or unfamiliar paths. Walking has the power to both enchant and lift enchantments. As you travel on your way, if you become aware that your chattering thoughts are burdensome, simply drop them by the wayside and walk on. Be mindful of the moment so you don't miss what is there.

When we walk on the Earth, our feet touch the ground, and we are moving through the sky. Often, when we think of the sky, we look up. However, the sky actually begins where the atmosphere touches the Earth, right where our feet meet the ground. So in this way we are truly "skywalkers."

The encouragement to "take your time," is worthwhile counsel. "Take" in this expression with time is interesting to think about. "Take" has several layers of meaning, i.e., lay hold of, receive, overcome.

Crawford Notch from Mt. Willard, New Hampshire

"You will go out in joy and be led forth in peace;
the mountains and hills will burst into song before you,
and all the trees of the field will clap their hands." —Isaiah 55:12

"The Little Cares"
—Elizabeth Barrett Browning

The little cares that fretted me,
I lost them yesterday
Among the fields above the sea,
Among the winds at play;
Among the lowing of the herds,
The rustling of the trees,
Among the singing of the birds,
The humming of the bees.

The foolish fears of what may happen—
I cast them all away
Among the clover-scented grass,
Among the new-mown hay;
Among the husking of the corn
Where drowsy poppies nod,
Where ill thoughts die and good are born,
Out in the fields with God.

"*...with God all things are possible.*"

—Matthew 19:26

Our hearts, through our feelings, will often reveal to us the reality of a universe in harmony; a coordinated, synchronized whole; a connectedness (unity) that many of us cannot enter into with our intellect alone, which sees (the world) in disconnected fragments. Think of progressing along your path in Nature, not as one of detachment like an ascetic, but as a mystic, toward union.

When you see a robin on the edge of the lawn, listening and watching, and you realize that he is, in fact, the essence of God in the guise of a small, feathered being, you realize that God is all encompassing, and that you are enveloped, enmeshed in a Divine Universe of which you are an integral and important component. You see the world more the way it is. You see a glimpse of reality uncloaked. You experience a taste of the Divinity of Nature.

"*...One God and Father of all, who is over all and through all and in all.*"

—Ephesians 4:6

Black Elk encourages us to experience the peace that finds its home in our souls when we awaken to the interconnectedness and unity with the universe. The Great Spirit is not just at the universe's core, but also permeates every facet of existence—within each and every one of us.

We have all noticed how rapidly time passes when we are caught up in the commotion of our daily lives. But when we move into Nature, deeply breathing and being breathed by all that surrounds us, it is as though we shift in time, moving closer to a centered place.

"*Within you there is a stillness and a sanctuary to which you can retreat and be yourself.*"

—Herman Hesse.

> *"I found I had less and less to say, until finally, I became silent, and began to listen. I discovered in the silence, the voice of God."*
> —Soren Kierkegaard

Nature Absorption is a way to leave the turmoil of yesterday and the problems of tomorrow, released from the whirl of our thoughts. Cross over the threshold, that which separates the outside from the inside, and step into Nature. It is like saying, "Here I am, God." Just as the Biblical Samuel, awakened by God, replied, "I am listening."

We are not alone, even in our solitude.

When we turn our attention toward the Natural World around us, we are drawn out of ourselves and into the present moment. There is an increase in awareness and a more intense sense of reality. We become unbound by the mental activity and emotional turmoil that so often overwhelm the senses and prevent a deep appreciation and awe of this Natural World and of our intricate participation and connection within it. As our *experience* with Nature increases, so does our awareness. As our *awareness* increases, so does our experience with Nature. As the cloth in India is dyed, we gain incrementally, and our ability to *be here now* naturally intensifies. This is the power of Nature Absorption.

There is a Divine living presence in the Natural World that resonates with the living spirit within each of us, unveiling our own relationship with God. There are many paths leading to the opening of ourselves to this transcendent spiritual connection. Birding with God is one easy, comfortable, efficient, and exciting path to Nature Absorption. When you are identifying, watching, or just feeding birds, you are never alone; you are always "Birding with God."

Yellow Warbler

"Invitation to Love"
—Paul Laurence Dunbar

Come when the nights are bright with stars
Or come when the moon is mellow;
Come when the sun his golden bars
Drops on the hay-field yellow.
Come in the twilight soft and gray,
Come in the night or come in the day,
Come, O love, whene'er you may,
And you are welcome, welcome.

You are sweet, O Love, dear Love,
You are soft as the nesting dove.
Come to my heart and bring it to rest
As the bird flies home to its welcome nest.

Come when my heart is full of grief
Or when my heart is merry;
Come with the falling of the leaf
Or with the redd'ning cherry.
Come when the year's first blossom blows,
Come when the summer gleams and glows,
Come with the winter's drifting snows,
And you are welcome, welcome.

SECTION II

Nature Encounters for Families

The simple adventures in this section are particularly designed for families. Children need time away from electronic devices and screens. It is important to have exposure to and time spent in this magnificent world in which we live. We all know the importance of fresh air, exercise, and sunlight, but a transformative awakening can be gained through Nature Absorption. These encounters, though simple, are enjoyable, informative, and beneficial for adults as well as children. When children and adults do these exercises together, the experience is enhanced, as each comes from a different perspective.

This section, including the poetry, is here to encourage children to look around and take notice of the many and varied aspects of the Natural World that surrounds them; to broaden their view, change their perspective, increase their awareness, and stimulate their innate imaginations and curiosity.

These encounters, with or without a child, are supportive and encouraging exercises in Nature Absorption.

"Memory"
—Thomas Bailey Aldrich

My mind lets go a thousand things,
Like dates of wars and deaths of kings,
And yet recalls the very hour—
'twas noon by yonder village tower,
And on the last blue moon in May—
The wind came briskly up this way,
Crisping the brook beside the road;

Then pausing here, set down its load
Of pine-scents, and shook listlessly
Two petals from that wild-rose tree.

Commit to spending a specific amount of time each week on planned experiences with Nature.

- Purpose: To increase your Nature Absorption and to develop greater awareness, joy, wonder, familiarity with and sense of connection and belonging to the Natural World.

- Suggested Time: About two hours a week, either all at one time or divided into multiple shorter experiences.

- Plan Ahead: Schedule this important time into your regular daily and weekly routines. However, do not hesitate to be spontaneous when time and circumstances allow.

Activities in Nature Absorption:

1. Repeat any exercise in this book often.
2. Take a long walk on a familiar street that you typically drive down and now see it for the first time.
3. Find a nature trail in your vicinity and go for a hike.
4. Go berry picking in the countryside.
5. Visit an orchard and go fruit picking. If the orchard offers a tour, take it.

Passing Through the Seasons

Song from "Pippa Passes"
—Robert Browning

The year's at the spring,
And day's at the morn;
Morning's at seven;
The hill-side's dew-pearl'd;
The lark's on the wing;
The snail's on the thorn;
God's in His heaven—
All's right with the world!

"Bed in Summer"
—Robert Louis Stevenson

In winter I get up at night
And dress by yellow candle-light.
In summer, quite the other way,
I have to go to bed by day.

I have to go to bed and see
The birds still hopping on the tree,
Or hear the grown-up people's feet
Still going past me in the street.

And does it not seem hard to you,
When all the sky is clear and blue,
And I should like so much to play,
To have to go to bed by day?

"The Hayloft"
—Robert Louis Stevenson

Through all the pleasant meadow-side
The grass grew shoulder-high,
Till the shining scythes went far and wide
And cut it down to dry.

Those green and sweetly smelling crops
They led the wagons home;
And they piled them here in mountain tops
For mountaineers to roam.

Here is Mount Clear, Mount Rusty-Nail,
Mount Eagle and Mount High; —
The mice that in these mountains dwell,
No happier are than I!

Oh, what a joy to clamber there,
Oh, what a place for play,
With the sweet, the dim, the dusty air,
The happy hills of hay!

"Autumn Fires"
—Robert Louis Stevenson

In the other gardens
    And all up the vale,
From the autumn bonfires
    See the smoke trail!

Pleasant summer over
    And all the summer flowers,
The red fire blazes,
    The grey smoke towers.

Sing a song of seasons!
    Something bright in all!
Flowers in the summer,
    Fires in the fall!

"No!"
—Thomas Hood

No sun—no moon!
No morn—no noon—
No dawn—
No sky—no earthly view—
No distance looking blue—
No road—no street—no "t'other side the way"—
No end to any Row—
No indications where the Crescents go—
No top to any steeple—
No recognitions of familiar people—
No courtesies for showing 'em—
No knowing 'em!
No traveling at all—no locomotion,
No inkling of the way—no notion—
"No go"—by land or ocean—
No mail—no post—
No news from any foreign coast—
No park—no ring—no afternoon gentility—
No company—no nobility—
No warmth, no cheerfulness, no healthful ease,
No comfortable feel in any member—
No shade, no shine, no butterflies, no bees,
No fruits, no flowers, no leaves, no birds,
November!

"I Heard a Bird Sing"
—Oliver Herford

I heard a bird sing
In the dark of December.
A magical thing
And sweet to remember.

"We are nearer to Spring
Than we were in September,"
I heard a bird sing
In the dark of December.

"The North Wind"
—Anonymous

The north wind doth blow,
And we shall have snow,
And what will the robin do then, Poor thing?
He'll sit in a barn,
And keep himself warm,
And hide his head under his wing, Poor thing!
The north wind doth blow,
And we shall have snow,
And what will the swallow do then, Poor thing?
Oh, do you not know
That he's off long ago,
To a country where he will find spring, Poor thing!
The north wind doth blow,
And we shall have snow,
And what will the dormouse do then, Poor thing?
Roll'd up like a ball
In his nest snug and small
He'll sleep till warm weather comes in, Poor thing!
The north wind doth blow,
And we shall have snow,
And what will the honey-bee do then, Poor thing?
In his hive he will stay
Till the cold is away
And then he'll come out in the spring, Poor thing!
The north wind doth blow,
And we shall have snow,
And what will the children do then, Poor things?
When lessons are done
They will skip, jump and run,
Until they have made themselves warm, Poor things!

"Beyond Winter"
—Ralph Waldo Emerson

Over the winter glaciers
I see the summer glow,
And through the wild-piled snowdrift
The warm rosebuds below.

Frankenstein Cliff, Crawford Notch, New Hampshire

"Adopt the pace of Nature: her secret is patience." —Ralph Waldo Emerson

Nature Encounter—An Insight into "Bio-Progression"

Read the children's book *The Mountain That Loved A Bird* by Alice McLerran.

This is a modern myth with a simple and beautiful lesson.

Note: Reading this book is helpful for children and will be enjoyable for adults before experiencing the activities that follow.

Activities:

1. Go outside and look for rock that has begun to be broken down by vegetation:
   - Rocks with moss and lichen growing on them
   - Brick and stone walls with flowers growing out of them
   - Sidewalks with grass and wildflowers growing up through the cracks
2. Look for birds' nests in trees, on houses, in barns, on poles, on ledges of buildings.
   - Remember never to disturb them in any way.
3. In springtime, watch for birds gathering materials for nest building.

Note: Different birds make different kinds of nests using different kinds of materials. Some nests are tiny while others are very large.

- They use anything that will work for them, but some typical nest materials are:

sticks	string
twigs	yarn
flat leaves	flower petals
needles	mud
bark	
grasses	
feathers	
twine	

Bird Nest

4. If there is a river somewhere in your vicinity, find out if it flows out of the heart of a mountain.

Note: In the White Mountains of Northern New Hampshire, in the Presidential Range, Mt. Washington dominates as the highest peak in the Northeast. Three rivers—the Cutler, the Ellis and the Ammonoosuc—all flow out of the solid-rock heart of the Mountain. They flow from above tree line, down the rocky surface into the woods on its lower slopes, traveling out into the surrounding green valleys and then on to the Atlantic Ocean. The Mountain also has beautiful alpine lakes nestled in rock, not too far from the summit, called the Lakes of the Clouds.

Chatham, New Hampshire

Changes in Perspectives

"Hurt No Living Thing"
—Christina Georgina Rossetti

Hurt no living thing:
Ladybird, nor butterfly,
Nor moth with dusty wing,
Nor cricket chirping cheerily,
Nor grasshopper so light of leap,
Nor dancing gnat, nor beetle fat,
Nor harmless worms that creep.

"Foreign Lands"
—Robert Louis Stevenson

Up into the cherry tree
Who should climb but little me?
I held the trunk with both my hands
And looked abroad in foreign lands.
I saw the next door garden lie,
Adorned with flowers, before my eye,
And many pleasant places more
That I had never seen before.
I saw the dimpling river pass
And be the sky's blue looking-glass;
The dusty roads go up and down
With people tramping in to town.
If I could find a higher tree
Farther and farther I should see,
To where the grown-up river slips
Into the sea among the ships,
To where the road on either hand
Lead onward into fairy land,
Where all the children dine at five,
And all the playthings come alive.

"The Swing"
—Robert Louis Stevenson

How do you like to go up in a swing,
    Up in the air so blue?
Oh, I do think it the pleasantest thing
Ever a child can do!

Up in the air and over the wall,
    Till I can see so wide,
Rivers and trees and cattle and all
    Over the countryside—

Till I look down on the garden green,
    Down on the roof so brown—
Up in the air I go flying again,
    Up in the air and down!

"I'm Glad"
—Unknown Author

I'm glad the sky is painted blue,
And the Earth is painted green,
With such a lot of nice fresh air
All sandwiched in between.

Moon

"Many men walk by day; few walk by night. It is a very different season..."
—Henry David Thoreau

Nature Encounter—Getting Acquainted with the Night

Go out into the night. Experience the darkness and avoid using your flashlights. Let your eyes adjust to "night vision" and you will find that on most nights much can be seen even without additional lighting. Seek out some places that are free from street or window lighting; go into the woods or a remote field for a view of the night sky.

> *"On all sides novelties present themselves. Instead of the sun, there are the moon and stars; instead of the wood-thrush, there is the whippoorwill; instead of butterflies in the meadows, fire-flies, winged sparks of fire!"*
>
> —Henry David Thoreau

"In the night the eyes are partly closed, or retire into the head. Other senses take the lead. The walker is guided as well by the sense of smell. Every plant and field and forest emits its odor now, swamp-pink in the meadow, and tansy in the road; and there is the peculiar dry scent of corn which has begun to show its tassels. The senses both of hearing and smelling are more alert."

—Henry David Thoreau

1. Go outside during a moonlit night. Be very, very quiet. Wait, watch, and listen for the sights and sounds of the night. If you choose a night of a bright or full moon, it can be a beautifully eerie and impressive experience. This is particularly breathtaking in winter, when the moon is riding high in the sky. (Extra bonus if there is snow on the ground!)

"The Moon, on the breast of the new-fallen snow,
Gave a lustre of midday to objects below"

—Clement Moore

If you see the moon and it is not full, and you wonder if it is waxing or waning, remember the word DOC.

D	O	C
Waxing toward Full	Full	Waning from Full

D: If the curve of the moon is on the right side as in the letter *D*, it is waxing toward the full.

O: Full moon

C: If the curve is on the left as in the letter *C*, it is waning from the full.

2. Go outside on a dark, moonless night.
   a. Bring a flashlight or headlamp, but do not turn it on right away; your eyes will adjust to the darkness.
   b. Hold your flashlight close to the side of your head at eye level if you don't have a headlamp.
   c. Be still and silent, listening for night sounds.
   d. When your light is on, keep one eye closed to maintain night vision.
   e. If you hear a sound, turn your head toward the sound and quickly switch on your light. If you are in luck, you may see the night critter who is making all the noise. You may see its *eyeshine*. Many animals have a special light-reflecting surface right behind the retina of their eyes. If they look up at your flashlight, their eyes will reflect the light and appear to glow. (Remember, your flashlight must be held beside your head at the level of your eyes.) Different animals have different colored eyeshine.
      After the critter scurries away, quickly switch off your light and get ready for your next sighting.
   f. If you lose your night vision at any time, shut your eyes, slowly count to ten, and slowly open your eyes. Your night vision should be restored quickly.
   g. If you do not hear or see any critters on a particular night, just enjoy the silence and the beauty of the adventure.

3. If you go out in the dark and you are not looking to catch a night critter's eyeshine with your flashlight, but you just want to prowl around exploring your environment at night, remember that a headlamp with its red light switched on will enable you to see without impairing your night vision.

Eastern Coyote, eyeshine

Night into Day

"The Star"
—Jane Taylor

Twinkle, twinkle, little star,
How I wonder what you are!
Up above the world so high,
Like a diamond in the sky.

When the blazing sun is gone,
When he nothing shines upon,
Then you show your little light,
Twinkle, twinkle, all the night.

Then the traveler in the dark
Thanks you for your tiny spark,
How could he see where to go,
If you did not twinkle so?

In the dark blue sky you keep,
Often through my curtains peep
For you never shut your eye,
Till the sun is in the sky.

As your bright and tiny spark
Lights the traveler in the dark,
Though I know not what you are,
Twinkle, twinkle, little star.

"The Moon"
—Robert Louis Stevenson

The moon has a face like the clock in the hall;
She shines on thieves on the garden wall,
On streets and fields and harbour quays,
And birdies asleep in the forks of the trees.

The squalling cat and the squeaking mouse,
The howling dog by the door of the house,
The bat that lies in bed at noon,
All love to be out by the light of the moon.

But all of the things that belong to the day
Cuddle to sleep to be out of her way;
And flowers and children close their eyes
Till up in the morning the sun shall arise.

"Dawn"
—Paul Laurence Dunbar

An angel, robed in spotless white,
Bent down and kissed the sleeping Night.
Night woke to blush; the sprite was gone.
Men saw the blush and called it Dawn.

"Daybreak"
—Henry Wadsworth Longfellow

A wind came up out of the sea,
And said, "O mists, make room for me."

It hailed the ships, and cried, "Sail on,
Ye mariners, the night is gone."

And hurried landward far away,
Crying, "Awake! it is the day."

It said unto the forest, "Shout!
Hang all your leafy banners out!"

It touched the wood-bird's folded wing,
And said, "O bird, awake and sing."

And o'er the farms, "O chanticleer,
Your clarion blow; the day is near."

It whispered to the fields of corn,
"Bow down, and hail the coming morn."

It shouted through the belfry-tower,
"Awake, O bell! proclaim the hour."

It crossed the churchyard with a sigh,
And said, "Not yet! in quiet lie."

Barred Owl, Chatham, New Hampshire

Nature Encounter—An Adventure with Owls

Read the children's book *Owl Moon* by Jane Yolen

Note: Reading this book is helpful for children and will be enjoyable for adults before experiencing the activities that follow.

Interesting facts about owls:

1. There are nearly two hundred species of owls in the world. They live on every continent except Antarctica.

2. Owls are raptors. They have four main characteristics:
   - They are carnivores.
   - They have excellent eyesight.
   - They have excellent hearing.
   - They have razor-sharp talons.

3. Owls are primarily nocturnal (hunting at night) but some do hunt during the day and at dusk and dawn.

4. Diets: Different owls have different diets.
    - They may eat: Squirrels, Skunks, Rabbits, Birds, Snakes, Insects, Rodents.
    - Owls eat a lot! A month-old owlet can eat up to four rodents a day. Some owls eat their own weight or more in a single night.

5. Eyesight: Owls' eyesight is excellent; a Great Horned Owl could detect the bottom line of an eye chart from a mile away! Their eyes are the same size as humans but their heads are the size of a baseball. An owl cannot turn its head all the way around, but it can turn its head 270 degrees and almost completely upside down. Its eyes are fixed in their sockets; an owl needs this flexibility in order to hunt. It has given up the muscles used for mobility in exchange for eye size.

6. Hearing: Owls have the sharpest hearing of all the birds on the planet. An owl can hear the heartbeat of its prey without a stethoscope. It can detect the footsteps of a mouse as it scuttles across the meadow. Owls' ears are disk-shaped areas on each side of their heads. They are covered by feathers which actually help focus the sound and make it clearer.

7. Hunting: Owls' ears are different from one another in size and position. One ear may be higher or larger than the other. By moving its head and adjusting so the volume in each asymmetrical ear is the same, the bird will be looking directly at its prey whether it can see it or not; an owl can tell precisely where its prey is located in low-light or no-light conditions. When an owl glides, its wings are as silent as smoke. Once the prey is located, the owl glides down from behind and grasps it with its talons, usually by the hindquarters. It then swallows it whole, head first.

8. Pellets: Owls do not chew their food; they do not have a crop for food storage, and what they eat goes directly into their gizzard,

the muscular portion of the bird's stomach. They cough up pellets containing everything they cannot digest. An owl pellet is a small, compressed bundle of bones, fur, feathers, and other inedible bits. The pellet is cast up by the owl and left behind. The owl is now ready to eat once again.

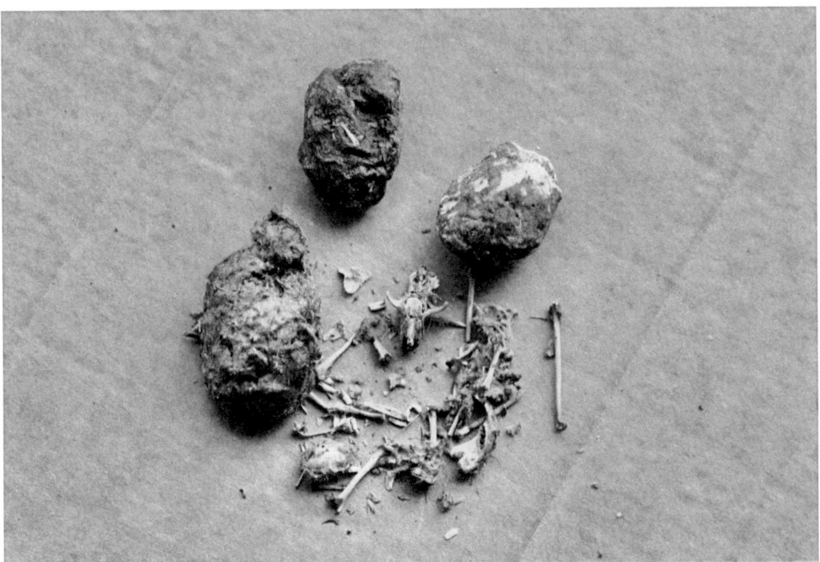

Owl pellets

Note: If you are ever lucky enough to find an owl pellet, take it home and carefully dissect it (tweezers help). See how much of the contents you can identify. You may be able to learn what the owl was eating that night. You possibly can reconstruct an entire skeleton. Often in the back of mammal identification guides there is a section with dental formulae that can be used to identify what the animal is using only its teeth and skull.

9. A "Parliament" is what a group of owls is sometimes called.

Activities:

1. Owling
   - Contact a nature center near you and ask about owling excursions that may be available to you.
   - If you practice "hooting," you can call in owls yourself. Each species has its own call, and some are easy to mimic. Perhaps you could gather some folks together, form an owling group and arrange for your own owling adventure. A rainy night or just after a rain is not good as the moist ground softens the sounds of prey, and the owls are not hunting.

Birds of a Feather

"Questioning Faces"
—Robert Frost

The winter owl banked just in time to pass
And save herself from breaking window glass.
And her wings straining suddenly aspread
Caught color from the last of evening red
In a display of underdown and quill
To glassed-in children at the window sill.

"A Wise Old Owl"
—Old English Nursery Rhyme

A wise old owl lived in an oak,
The more he saw, the less he spoke
The less he spoke, the more he heard,
Why aren't we all like that wise old bird?

"The Woodpecker"
—Elizabeth Madox Roberts

The woodpecker pecked out a little round hole
And made him a house in the telephone pole.
One day when I watched he poked out his head,
And he had on a hood and a collar of red.
When the streams of rain pour out of the sky,
And the sparkles of lightning go flashing by,
And the big, big wheels of thunder roll,
He can snuggle back in the telephone pole.

Bird Nouns of Assemblage

Bevy of quail
Bouquet of pheasants
Building of rooks
Clamor of rooks
Cast of hawks
Kettle of hawks
Circus of puffins
Charm of finches
Charm of hummingbirds
Chime of wrens
Cluster of knots
Commotion of coot
Convocation of Eagles
Covert of coot
Congregation of plover
Dule of doves
Exaltation of larks
Fall of woodcock
Gulp of cormorants
Herd of curlews
Bevy of swans
Screw of soaring birds
Murder of crows
Murmuration of starlings
Muster of storks
Ostentation of peacocks
Pack of grouse
Paddling of ducks
Parliament of owls
Peep of chickens
Pitying of doves
Raft of ducks
Rafter of turkeys
Richness of martins
Siege of bitterns
Siege of herons
Gaggle of geese
Skein of geese (in flight)
Spring of teal
Stand of flamingos
Flamboyance of flamingos
Strand of silky flycatchers
Tiding of magpies
Unkindness of ravens
Walk of snipe
Wisp of snipe
Watch of nightingales
Wake of vultures

Turkey Vulture

Nature Encounter—Getting to Know the Wind

Read: The Children's Book *What Makes the Wind?* by Laurence Santrey

Note: Reading this book is helpful for children and will be enjoyable for adults before experiencing the activities that follow.

Activities:

1. Go fly a kite!
   - Suggestions for kite flying on a windy day:
     a. Be sure to find an open space far from electrical wires.
     b. Choose a place that is generally windy, such as a park, a large school playground, a sandy beach, an open field, or a school athletic field.

c. Find directions online for making your own kite.
d. Be sure to have plenty of lightweight string (bring extra string). If you are having good luck and your kite is up and flying high, when you come to the end of your ball of string, tie on a new one. See just how high your kite will fly.

2. Walk in the wind
   - Go outside on a blustery day and experience the wind; feel it blowing on your face and through your hair.

3. Hang a windsock
   - A windsock is a cone-shaped tube, usually made of nylon material. It resembles a giant sock without the foot part. It is used as a basic guide to wind direction and speed. Hang it outside where it can be seen from inside the house. You can find online directions for making your own.

4. Practice becoming familiar with the Four Winds: North, South, East and West.
   - Winds are named for the direction they are coming *from*. When the East Wind blows, does it bring the salty scent of sea air? Is it usually cool and damp? When it blows hard, is it raw and chilling? Or where you live, is the East Wind warm and pleasant. Perhaps it brings the wonderful scents of the bakery down the block.

5. Remember: March is the windy month.

Blowing in the Wind...the Breath of Heaven

"Who Has Seen the Wind?"
—Christina Rossetti

Who has seen the wind?
Neither I nor you:
But when the leaves hang trembling,
The wind is passing through.

Who has seen the wind?
Neither you nor I:
But when the trees bow down their heads,
The wind is passing by.

"Little Wind"
—Kate Greenaway

Little wind, blow on the hill top;
Little wind, blow down the plain;
Little wind, blow up the sunshine;
Little wind, blow off the rain.

"The Wind"
—Robert Louis Stevenson

I saw you toss the kites on high
And blow the birds about the sky;
And all around I heard you pass,
Like ladies' skirts across the grass—
O wind, a-blowing all day long,
O wind, that sings so loud a song!

I saw the different things you did,
But always you yourself you hid.
I felt you push, I heard you call,
I could not see yourself at all—
O wind, a-blowing all day long,
O wind, that sings so loud a song!

O you that are so strong and cold,
O blower, are you young or old?
Are you a beast of field and tree,
Or just a stronger child than me?
O wind, a-blowing all day long,
O wind, that sings so loud a song!

"What the Winds Bring"
—Edmund Clarence Stedman

Which is the Wind that brings the cold?
The North-Wind, Freddy, and all the snow;
And the sheep will scamper into the fold
When the North begins to blow.

Which is the Wind that brings the heat?
The South-Wind, Katy, and corn will grow,
And peaches redden for you to eat,
When the South begins to blow.

Which is the Wind that brings the rain?
The East-Wind, Arty; and farmers know
That cows come shivering up the lane
When the East begins to blow.

Which is the Wind that brings the flowers?
The West-Wind, Bessy; and soft and low
The birdies sing in the summer hours
When the West begins to blow.

Clouds

Nature Encounter—Getting to Know Clouds

Read: The children's book *The Cloud Book* by Tomie de Paola

Note: Reading this book is helpful for children and will be enjoyable for adults before experiencing the activities that follow.

Activities:

1. Take *The Cloud Book* outside and observe the sky, using the book to identify the clouds.

2. Keep a small daily "cloud log" and record your observations. Throughout your day, take note of the cloud formations and what weather they may indicate. Using their simple names at first may be very helpful.
   a. Example: Monday, June 6, 2023, 10:00 a.m.: Mares' Tails—a change in the weather is coming.
   b. Refer to your earlier accounts and see if the clouds' indications (and your interpretations) were accurate.

3. Use your imagination to find what creatures and objects you may see in the shapes of the clouds.

4. You may want to expand your "cloud log" into a weather journal.

5. Remember to keep looking up!

Drifting with the Clouds

"Clouds"
—Anonymous

Scattered and wispy clouds in the sky…
Cirrus clouds are drifting by.

Long and flat clouds in the sky…
Stratus clouds are moving by.

Large and puffy clouds in the sky…
Cumulus clouds are floating by.

High and dark clouds in the sky…
Cumulonimbus clouds are thundering by.

"Clouds"
—Christina Georgina Rossetti

White sheep, white sheep,
On a blue hill,
When the wind stops,
You all stand still.
When the wind blows,
You walk away slow.
White sheep, white sheep,
Where do you go?

"What's Floating By"
—Anonymous

What's fluffy and white and floats up high?
    Like a pile of cotton in the sky?
And when the wind blows hard and strong,
    What very gently floats along?

What brings the rain, what brings the snow?
    What showers down on us below?
When you look up high in the sky,
    What is that thing you see floating by?

Atlantic Puffin, Drangey Island, Iceland

Nature Encounter—Keeping a Weather Journal

> *"Sunshine is delicious, rain is refreshing, wind braces me up, snow is exhilarating; there is really no such thing as bad weather, only different kinds of good weather."*
>
> —John Ruskin

Taking notice of the weather keeps us mindful of our connection with the Natural World. Keeping a weather journal will help you be attentive to what is happening during the course of the day and how it may be affecting you and all of Nature around you.

Your weather journal can be as simple or as detailed as you like. You do not need to know the names of the various types of clouds to begin noting their shape, color, and size. You do not need to know the names of the winds to note the wind's direction and strength. You do not even need a thermometer to record the exact temperature; simply note the "cool morning" or the "warmer afternoon." You may find over time that you begin to associate different clouds and winds with changing weather. Try to note the general *feel* of the moment, both physical and emotional: Is it muggy, sticky, dry, oppressive, fresh, invigorating?

The weather is continually changing throughout the course of the day, with variations in temperature, sky conditions, humidity, wind, and air pressure. The sun heats the Earth's surface unevenly, and its intensity varies from one time of day to another. Often mornings and evenings are cooler, with the hottest time of day being midafternoon (usually between two and four o'clock). Earth transmits the heat it has absorbed from the sun into the air, and when this warm air rises higher into the atmosphere, it cools down. All air contains some water vapor, and as the warm air cools, the water vapor turns into tiny droplets of water or ice, which accumulate and form clouds.

Clouds play a major role in our daily weather. They determine how much of the sun's rays reach Earth during the day, and at night how much of Earth's heat gets released back into space. Wind is another key player in our daily weather. Wind propels the clouds, moving water vapor and creating temperature variations.

There is more to *feeling* the day than just the temperature. You may think you only feel the air when the wind blows, but your body actually *feels* the air around you all the time. Air has weight and it is constantly pressing against you, along with everything else it touches. Air pressure is caused by Earth's gravity pulling air downward. "High Pressure" occurs when cold air pushes down, usually bringing fair weather. "Low Pressure" occurs when warm air rises up to make clouds and rain. With a change in temperature, there is also a change in air pressure. When air pressure decreases, the temperature decreases; and when air pressure increases, the temperature increases. Our body (tissue, blood vessels), as well as our emotions, react to changes in air pressure, temperature, humidity, cloud cover, and wind. Many people have lost the awareness of the day's weather, but obviously flora and fauna are sensitive and reactive to even subtle changes in the atmosphere.

Simply by paying attention, you will begin to have a greater sense of the day's weather changes and an increased awareness of the Natural World around you. It is best to record your observations (temperature, sky conditions, wind) at a few regular intervals during the day; perhaps start with morning, midday, afternoon, and evening, and include notes or thoughts about how and what you are feeling. This can be done with a child or individually, and you can compare your journals at the end of the day or week.

Atlantic Puffin

It's Raining, It's Pouring

"The Rain Has Silver Sandals"
—May Justus

The rain has silver sandals
For dancing in the spring,
And shoes with golden tassels
For summer's frolicking.
Her winter boots have hobnails
Of ice from heel to toe,
Which now and then she changes
For moccasins of snow.

"Rain"
—Robert Louis Stevenson

The rain is raining all around,
It falls on field and tree,
It rains on the umbrellas here,
And on the ships at sea.

"Mud"
—Polly Chase Boyden

Mud is very nice to feel
All squishy-squash between the toes!
I'd rather wade in wiggly mud
Than smell a yellow rose.

Nobody else but the rosebush knows
How nice mud feels
Between the toes.

Red Oak, Chatham, New Hampshire

"Everybody needs beauty as well as bread, places to play in and pray in, where nature may heal and give strength to body and soul." —John Muir

Nature Encounters—Making the Woods Your Own

Since the earliest of time, people of all cultures have been making up wonderful stories about the world around them. These ancient tales often explained different aspects of natural phenomena for which humans, at that time, had no scientific explanation.

These myths and legends show a keen interest in and deep awareness of the workings of the Natural World.

As people who lived very close to the Earth, early folks were directly affected by all aspects of Nature in the places where they dwelled. Today, we are less directly affected, much more removed. As a result, we have lost much of our awareness and connection.

Children are natural storytellers. They are constantly creating vibrant stories during their play and activities. Storytelling is a process for bringing an *outward* experience *within*. Children, as well as adults, can develop a deeper awareness of and closer connection to our Natural World and the cosmos beyond by creating their own myths and legends of explanation. The following are three modern examples of this.

Mooseltoe

The Legend of Mooseltoe—S.M.F.

In a long-ago time, the Great Sylvan Spirit of the North Woods, lord of the trees and the waters, lived in harmony with all within his realm.

Once, in the dark time of a year, a shadowed spirit from the sea swept across the North Woods in the form of a great storm. He was jealous of the Great Spirit's position and of the love and devotion given him. The dark spirit sought to rob this lord of many of his mighty and beautiful trees and to wash away his lovely streams with great floods. He wished to give these things to the Lord of the Sea as a gift in order to gain favor for his own dark ends. Now a singing stream had heard the whispers of his evil plan as she tarried by the sea. Swiftly, she sent word up her waters to warn the Great Spirit of the North Woods so that he might protect his trees and all that sheltered under them. But the Winds blew strong and the creatures were already taking cover. And so gentle was her voice that none heard, none but one small, young deer who stopped to drink from the singing waters. Hearing the alarm, he bravely carried the message through the forest to the Great Spirit, who then summoned all his powers and secured those of other spirits friendly to him. He successfully protected his realm from the storm ravages of the shadowed spirit from the sea.

To reward their courage, the Great Spirit made the little stream a mighty river, and he gave a special blessing to the little deer and to all his children to come. He bestowed on them great strength, endurance, and prosperity. And so, the stalwart Moose came into being. And he was given guardianship over all the forest lands.

And to this day, folks hang his woody droppings, *especially in the dark time of the year*, as a symbol of honor to the brave Moose that he might protect their homes from storms and shadowed spirits and to gain for them the good graces of the Great Spirit of the North Woods.

The Legend of Balsam—S.M.F

Once in a time long ago, the North Woods was preparing for the coming of Winter. As Autumn grew older, snow flurries filled the air, and the evening cold spread layers of thin ice across the ponds. Yet, the Forest was savoring those last, sweet, lingering moments when the Sun's light still filled the Woods with brightness and with warmth. On a day such as this, the Wind came swirling through the trees in a frenzy, seeking the whereabouts of the Guardian Moose, Steward of the Great Lord of the North Woods. The Wind bore him an urgent and ominous message. A bitter Cold was on the march, moving down from the far reaches of the North. And Darkness and Hunger followed after him. These three, wishing to extend their Kingdoms, wanted to claim the Forest for their own and to hold reign over it forever. Spring never returns to lands within their grasp.

The Moose was gravely troubled by these ill tidings. At once he sought the council of the Great Lord who said, "These are forces too powerful for even me alone. I shall travel south and find Spring. If I can persuade her to come back with me and aid us in our peril—perhaps we shall win this battle.

"Make haste, Moose. There can be no delay. Everything in the Forest must take winter shelter swiftly. For even if we win this struggle and push these bitter forces back beyond our borders, all living things who succumb to them shall be carried back to the Far Reaches and shall never be seen in our land again. For it is lonely there, and they long for living things. They will not easily retreat without some prizes won."

Snow was deepening upon the ground. A fierce and eerie Wind blew cold. The Moose dearly loved Winter. He, above all creatures here, was blessed with greater abilities to withstand its hardships. He traveled throughout the forest urging all to shelter themselves quickly and keep in store enough nourishment to support them for some time to come, that all might be readied to withstand the coming onslaught. Tirelessly, the valiant Moose kept his faithful vigil, ever watchful for those who needed his skillful help. Alas, the White-tailed Deer and the Snowshoe Hare had not found refuge in time. The storming had already begun when the Moose found them, shaking with hunger and with fear. He comforted them and began to search for shelter. He called to all the Forest to help them so they might not be lost from the North Woods forever. Few heard above the wailing of the Wind. But a little grove of scrubby Fir bushes, growing unnoticed close to the ground, called back, "Father Moose, give them to us. We are small but we shall guard them with our very lives. We shall bend our branches over them, and when they are hungry, they may eat upon our needles." And this they did.

The Moose continued to watch over the Woods, traveling far and wide. Often, he would stop to rest and take sustenance with the little Fir bushes, browsing upon their evergreen needles and deeply grateful for their steadfast help. Throughout the onslaught, the woody, winter droppings of the Moose were everywhere in the forest. Seeing them, all his folk took heart and endured, knowing that the Moose was abroad, always caring for and protecting them. Whatever might come to pass, all was well.

When the ordeal was over, and the Cruel Forces sent back from whence they'd come, the Forest began to awaken to spring and to healing.

The Great Lord, Sylvan Spirit of the North Woods, made a decree. He spoke to the little, brave fir scrubs, now weakened and broken by their toil and efforts on behalf of others. "Such compassion will never go unrewarded. You shall be known henceforth as the Balsam Fir, and you shall grow tall and beautiful. And so that your brave and kindly deeds shall never be forgotten, the scent of your needles shall be exquisite and shall fill the Forest air. And this scent shall ever be recognized as the Scent of the North Woods. And together with the woody droppings of the Stalwart Moose shall be held as a symbol of Faithfulness, Compassion, and Courage."

Retelling of an American Indian Legend—S.M.F.

In a far distant time, an American Indian tribe lived in peace and harmony with its surroundings and with each other. All were content and faithfully abided by the laws of their ancient and wise fathers. Their chief was well-respected and loved, for he was a just man and took good care of the people.

There was at this time a strong, young brave who displayed many fine qualities. The people were proud of his accomplishments, and he was cherished by all, particularly by their good chief who had long been watching him grow into manhood with the hope that he would become the next chief when the time came.

Early one summer, when this noble brave was hunting for food for the people, he spotted a large stag moving slowly through the forest. The young brave held his breath and stealthily followed, readying his bow as he moved cautiously along. While taking careful aim, in one perfect moment, he let his arrow fly. It reached the stag with keen precision and in an instant, he fell to the ground, lifeless.

The brave looked up with joy at his success; but in the next moment, his joy was consumed by horror and by shame. He was stricken by the realization that both he and the stag had wandered unknowingly into the sacred forest burial grounds of his ancestors.

Everyone was aware of the strict law—never was there to be hunting in that holy place, and the penalty for transgression was death. He fell to his knees in pain and remorse. Slowly, he rose and headed back to the village where he sought the benevolent chief in order to confess his tragic mistake.

The good chief's heart was breaking as he pronounced to the people, that in spite of the innocence of the error, this young brave must die, for that was the sacred law by which they lived.

Now it happened that a lovely, young maiden loved the brave dearly. She had hoped that one day they would wed. She went to the chief and pleaded and begged for the life of her beloved. It seemed to no avail. Everyone was in deep despair.

Then the chief remembered that he alone could set the hour of the fateful death. That was one of the responsibilities passed down to him from his forefathers. He told the tearful maiden that he could not change the fatal destiny of her beloved, but he could prolong his life awhile. He declared that when all the trees of the forest had dropped all their leaves, then the brave must die. This would give them all summer and late into the fall.

As the sad and painful time grew closer, and the trees were preparing to drop their leaves, the young maiden went tearfully throughout the forest, pleading with all the trees to hold tight to their leaves for the sake of her beloved. It seemed that none were listening, for they continued to prepare for winter, and their leaves fell fast, then faster. When late fall drew nigh and most trees were already bare, the maiden and all the people were suffering from grief and hopelessness.

As the chill winds of winter began to blow and snow was in the air, someone noticed that the leaves of the stately Oaks and the lovely Beeches were brown and dry, but somehow still clinging to the branches of these trees. Could it be? Could the Oak and the Beech trees have heard the maiden's plea? The people watched with wonder and were afraid to hope. Yet, winter came, and still the leaves did not fall.

In the spring, the people and the forest rejoiced with happiness beyond description; for new leaves appeared as the withered leaves fell. Henceforth, these kind trees held onto their leaves every winter until their new ones appeared each spring. So, the fine young brave's life was spared because these good trees alone had listened.

American Beech in winter

Termite Mound, Lake Manyara National Park, Tanzania
"Of all the paths you take in life, make sure a few of them are dirt." —John Muir

Epilogue

No matter where we are, Nature is there, all around us, within and without, seeking our attention. We need a different perspective to hear this calling. A change of perspective leads to a change in perception.

Nature Absorption is a path of intuition, healing, and spiritual transformation. Enter into the Natural World in order for the energies, the power of Nature, to enter into you.

Journey into the world of Nature, the world of the obscure, the world of the ordinary, the world of ourselves and our awesome planet and see what it may hold. You can choose…the miracles are happening now…we are very much a part of them.

We are all travelers here on Earth, which is itself a traveler in the solar system, on a voyage through our Milky Way Galaxy, all proceeding on our way in the cosmos. There are life-changing adventures to be had.

About the Authors

Chris Lewey, Executive Director and Founder of RAVEN Interpretive Programs, holds a Master's in Environmental Studies from Antioch University and attended Maharishi European Research University in France. He studied The Science of Creative Intelligence and Transcendental Meditation with Maharishi Mahesh Yogi and has continued the practice of TM for over fifty years. Chris has led tours and programs for RAVEN, as well as such organizations as the Maine Audubon Society, Smithsonian Study Tours, Road Scholar, Tauck World Discovery, and the National Wildlife Federation. Chris has led many overnight EduTrips for the Mount Washington Observatory to the summit of the Northeast's highest peak, home of "the world's worst weather." He has taught ornithology for the National Audubon Society at their Hog Island ecology camp on the coast of Maine, where he was the Director of their Joy of Birding and Breaking into Birding programs for many years. A native New Englander and licensed Maine Guide, he has taught biology, ecology, and ornithology in both New Hampshire and Maine. RAVEN offers historical and ecological insights into the diverse environs of Northern New England, Canada, the American West, Hawaii, Alaska, and beyond. Chris personally leads many trips and has traveled extensively from Alaska to Eastern Canada, South America to the Antarctic peninsula, Arctic Greenland, Europe and East Africa. He is a well-known lecturer to the largest travel companies in the world and personally gives over a hundred lectures a year for Tauck World Discovery, Globus Tours, Trafalgar Tours, Insight

Vacations, and several smaller travel companies, as well as to local schools, libraries, and nature centers. RAVEN leads birding outings and nature walks, as well as day trips and group tours. Chris has appeared on several radio and television programs including Animal Planet's *The Most Extreme* series, Maine Public Television's *Quest* nature series and ABC's *Good Morning America*. As a nature photographer and licensed master bird-bander he continues to enthusiastically share his perspectives and interesting interpretations of the Natural World. He has lived off the electrical grid at RAVEN's base in Chatham, New Hampshire, for over thirty years. Chris built the passive solar, energy-efficient structure that uses solar PV for electricity and super insulation for an efficient, high performing home and business. He shares his green home with his wife, two teenage boys, eight-year-old daughter, and three Labrador retrievers.

S.M. Fisher began her teaching career with a degree in history and a secondary school certification. However, one summer in Boston, having become involved in the administration of a Massachusetts state-wide educational program for very young, special needs children, her career took a major change in direction. With additional training and a second certification in elementary education, her work with young children began. Her career spanned forty years of teaching in a variety of situations, including both public and private schools. She works for RAVEN Interpretive Programs in a number of capacities. She developed walking tours for historic places, acts as an interpretive guide, and presents ecological slide programs of the White Mountains. She lives with her family in the White Mountains of Western Maine.

J.K. Lounsbury left the Boston area to travel through Europe in the late sixties. Living and working in Manchester, England; Madrid, Spain; and Davos Dorf, Switzerland; allowed her world perspective to be intimately shaped by many cultures and natural environments. After returning to the States and perching for a time within easy reach of the Rocky Mountains in Denver, Colorado, Jane migrated East, back home to her native New England. She has over forty years' administrative experience in a variety of fields, including RAVEN Interpretive Programs. She assisted with the development of, and participated in, RAVEN's wildlife trips and educational workshops. She now lives with her family on the "quiet side" of the White Mountains.

More information about RAVEN Interpretive Programs can be found at www.ravenprograms.com and on Facebook.

Credits

"Questioning Faces" by Robert Frost from THE POETRY OF ROBERT FROST edited by Edward Connery Lathem. Copyright © 1969 by Henry Holt and Company. Copyright © 1962 by Robert Frost. Reprinted by permission of Henry Holt and Company. All Rights Reserved.

Excerpt from "Two Tramps in Mud Time" by Robert Frost from THE POETRY OF ROBERT FROST edited by Edward Connery Lathem. Copyright © 1969 by Henry Holt and Company. Copyright © 1936 by Robert Frost, copyright © 1964 by Lesley Frost Ballantine. Reprinted by permission of Henry Holt and Company. All Rights Reserved.

Rumi quotes and poems, from the book *Rumi: The Beloved Is You* by Shahram Shiva, are used with the permission of Rumi Network.

Photography by Chris Lewey. All Rights Reserved.